Europe Made Easy
Travel Guides

Andy Herbach

Europe Made Easy
Travel Guides

www.eatndrink.com

MADRID MADE EASY
2020
ISBN: 9781661399801
–All Rights Reserved–

Acknowledgments
English editor: Marian Modesta Olson
Maps from designmaps.com
Contributor: Karl Raaum
Photos from Shutterstock, Pixabay, and Karl Raaum. Plaza de la Villa: Dalbera (Paris), Plaza Santa Ana: Sjaak Kempe, Museo de America and Teatro Real: Carlos Delgado

ABOUT THE AUTHOR

Andy Herbach is the author of the *Eating & Drinking* series of menu translators and restaurant guides, including *Eating & Drinking in Paris, Eating & Drinking in Italy, Eating & Drinking in Spain and Portugal*, and *Eating & Drinking in Latin America*. He is also the author of several travel guides, including *Paris Walks, Europe Made Easy, Paris Made Easy, Amsterdam Made Easy, Berlin Made Easy, Barcelona Made Easy, Italy Made Easy, Oslo Made Easy, French Riviera Made Easy* and *Provence Made Easy.* Andy is a lawyer and resides in Palm Springs, California.

You can e-mail him corrections, additions, and comments at eatndrink@aol.com or through his website at www.eatndrink.com.

TABLE OF CONTENTS

1. Introduction   7

2. Top Sights   11

3. Sights   23
A Day in Madrid   24
A Weekend in Madrid   31
A Week in and Around Madrid   38
  Churches & Religious Art   38
  Museum Day   43
  Northeast Madrid   50
  Northwest Madrid   54
  Toledo   59
  El Escorial Monastery   65
  The Valley of the Fallen   68

4. Walks   70
  Major Sights Walk I   71
  Major Sights Walk II   77
  Tapas Walk   80

5. Sleeping & Eating   83
  Sleeping   84
  Eating   87

6. Activities   93
  Shopping   93
  Nightlife and Entertainment   95
  Sports and Recreation   96

7. Planning Your Trip   97
  Getting Around Madrid   97
  Practical Matters   98
  Essential Phrases   103

8. Index   106

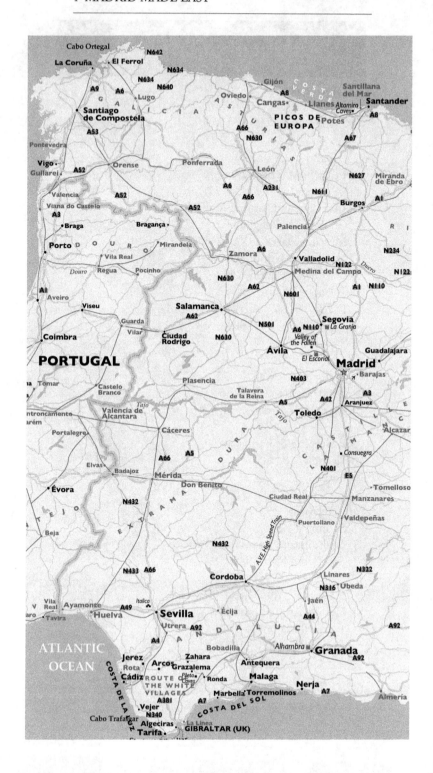

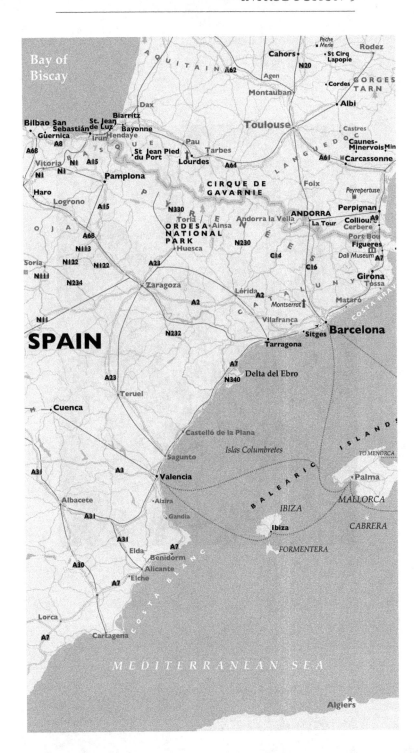

MAPS

Europe 1
Spain 4-5
Madrid 8-9
Major Sights 14-15
A Day in Madrid 25
Churches and Religious Art 39
Museums 44
Northeast Madrid 51
Northwest Madrid 55
Toledo 60
Excursions 66
Major Sights Walk I 72
Major Sights Walk II 73
Tapas Walk 81

1. INTRODUCTION

Madrid is Spain's capital city. It's not only located in the center of the country, it *is* the center of Spain. Although travelers come to visit Madrid's main attractions—including the fantastic Prado Museum—they soon get caught up in the city's lively nightlife. The *tapas* scene alone is worth the trip. Although you'll find plenty of new buildings, you'll also find Baroque and neo-Classical structures such as the Plaza Mayor (where it seems at times that everyone in Madrid is visiting) and the grand Palacio Real (Royal Palace).

If you have only a few days, we'll make it easy for you to truly experience Madrid. Our walks are designed for you to see the most sights in the shortest time.

So forget those large, bulky travel books. This handy little guide to Madrid is all you need to make your visit enjoyable, memorable—*and easy.*

8 MADRID MADE EASY

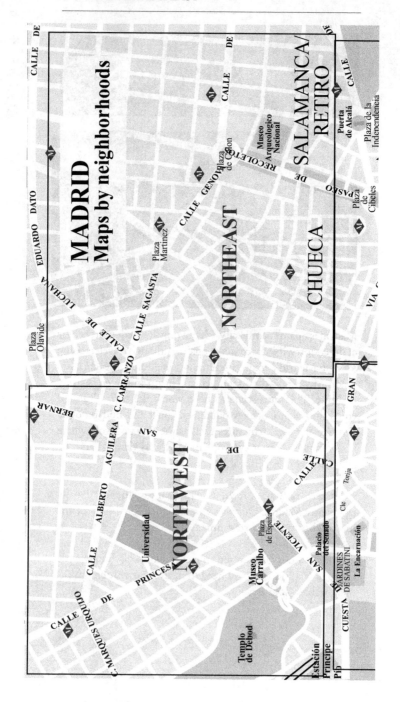

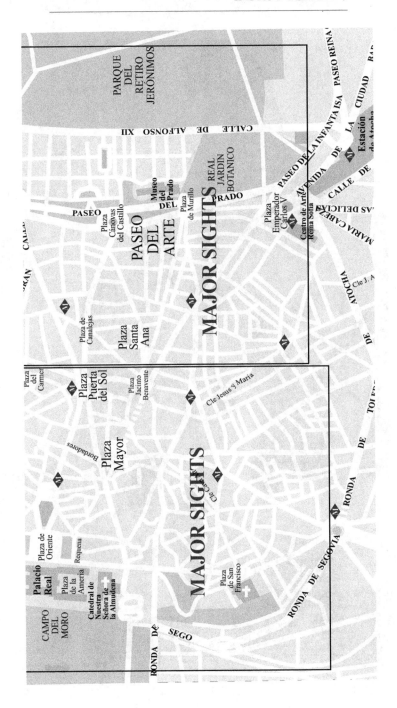

2. MADRID TOP SIGHTS

- **Palacio Real** (Royal Palace)
Spain's lavish national palace.
- **Museo Prado** (Prado Museum)
One of Europe's greatest museums.
- **Centro de Arte Reina Sofía**
Modern-art museum featuring Picasso's masterpiece *Guernica*.
- **Real Ermita de San Antonio de la Florida**
Goya's "Sistine Chapel."
- **Museo Thyssen-Bornemisza**
Interesting and eclectic art collection.
- **Plaza Mayor**
One of Europe's grandest squares.
- **El Retiro**
A vast and beautiful green space in the midst of the city.
- **Puerta del Sol**
Madrid's lively central square.
- **Convento de las Descalzas Reales**
An incredible collection of tapestries and paintings.
- **Museo de América**
Europe's best collection of pre-Columbian, Spanish-American, and Native American artifacts.
- **Plaza de Toros de las Ventas**
Attending a bullfight (*corrida*) here is the quintessential Spanish experience.
- **Catedral de Nuestra Señora de la Almudena**
Madrid's massive cathedral.
- **Plaza de la Villa**
The city's oldest square.
- **Teatro Real**
The elegant Royal Theater.
- **Plaza Santa Ana**
An excellent place to sample *tapas*.

You're going to experience the wonderful city of Madrid by visiting the top sights. There's something for everyone in this incredible city. From fabulous architecture to great museums to the lively *tapas* scene. Get ready to experience one of Europe's best destinations!

Palacio Real (Royal Palace)
Perched on a hill overlooking the city, the **Palacio Real** (Royal Palace) has 3,000 rooms, and some are open to the public. Spaniards will proudly tell you that it's twice as large as Buckingham Palace. The present building dates back to 1738, and is built on the sight of a former Moorish fortress. King Philip V wanted a palace similar to Versailles. Philip was the grandson of France's Louis XIV and was brought up at Versailles. Philip's son Charles III spent some of his youth in Italy and he added much of the sumptuous Italian interior. In 1762, Charles hired Giambattista Tiepolo to decorate three of the palace's rooms, including the Throne Room. Tiepolo spent four years creating elaborate ceiling frescoes. Over the years, each Spanish king expanded the palace trying to outdo his predecessor. Don't miss the Painting Gallery (filled with pieces by such notables as Velázquez and Goya), the Throne Room, the Reception Room and the Royal Armoury. You can also visit the rooms of King Alfonso XIII, who was the last resident until he abdicated in 1931. The elaborate Changing of the Guard takes place in the courtyard at noon on the first Wednesday of every month. *Info: Tel. 914548700. Open daily 10am-6pm (until 8pm Apr-Sep). Admission: €10, €5 ages 5-16. Metro: Ópera. www.patrimonionacional.es.*

Museo del Prado (Prado Museum)

The Museo del Prado (Prado Museum) is one of Europe's greatest museums, with 7,000 paintings (1,500 are on display at any one time) by such biggies as Velázquez, Goya, El Greco, Titian, Botticelli, Murillo and Rubens. A few Prado highlights are:

- *Garden of Love* by Rubens
- *Immaculate Conception* by Murillo
- *Martyrdom of St. Philip* by Ribera
- *The Annunciation* by Fra Angélico
- *Phillip II* by Titian
- *The Hay Cart* by Bosch
- *St. Peter Crucified Appearing to Peter Nolasco* by Zurbarán
- *Adam and Eve* by Dürer
- *Third of May* by Goya
- *Christ Carrying the Cross* by El Greco
- *The Maids of Honor (Las Meninas)* by Velázquez
- *David and Goliath* by Caravaggio

For many, the most stunning paintings here are Goya's late-life dark and disturbing Black Paintings, especially *Saturn Devouring One of His Sons*. *Info: Paseo del Prado. Tel. 913302880. Open: Mon-Sat 10am-8pm, Sun and holidays 10am-7pm. Closed Jan1, May 1, and Dec 25. Reduced hours Jan 6, May 1, Dec 24, and Dec 31 10am-2pm. Admission: €15. €7.50 students 18-25 and over 65. Under 18 free. Free Mon-Sat 6pm-8pm and Sun 5pm-7pm. Metro: Banco de España or Atocha. www.museodelprado.es.*

14 MADRID MADE EASY

Madrid Major Sights
1. Catedral
2. El Retiro
3. Jardín Botánico
4. Museo del Prado
5. Museo Thyssen-Bornemisza
6. Palacio Real
7. Plaza de la Villa
8. Plaza Mayor
9. Plaza Santa Ana
10. Puerta del Sol
11. Reina Sofía
12. Teatro Real

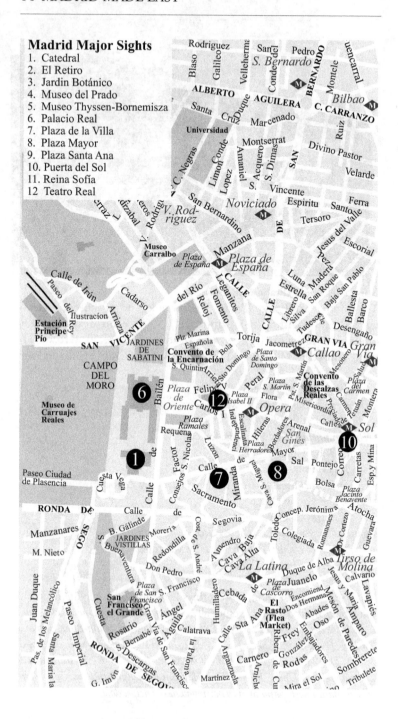

TOP SIGHTS 15

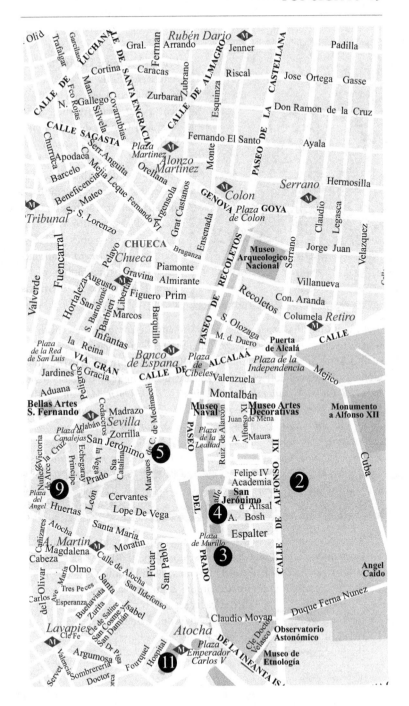

Museo Nacional Centro de Arte Reina Sofía

If you're interested in 20th-century art, come to the Museo Nacional Centro de Arte Reina Sofía. This contemporary art museum is housed in an 18th-century building that once was a hospital. There is an emphasis on 20th-century Spanish artists such as Picasso, Miró and Dalí. It's most famous painting is Picasso's masterpiece, *Guernica*, an anti-war painting of the bombing of the town of Guernica by the Germans during the Spanish Civil War. The museum also has a spectacular new wing, and there are great views from the transparent exterior elevators. The Reina Sofía collection has works by artists such as Antoni Tàpies, Jorge Oteiza, Julio Romero de Torres, Joan Miró, Julio González, Luis Gordillo, José Gutiérrez Solana, Lucio Muñoz, and Pablo Serrano. *Info: 52 Calle de Santa Isabel. Tel. 917741000. Open Mon and Wed-Sat 10am-9pm, Sun 10am-7pm. Closed Tue. Free Mon and Wed-Sat 7pm-9pm and Sun 1:30pm-7pm. (only a portion of the museum is open during free admission). Closed Jan 1, Jan 6, May 1, May 15, Nov 9, Dec 25 and Dec 31. Admission: €10. www. museoreinasofia.es.*

Paseo del Arte Ticket

The Paseo del Arte ticket allows entry to the **Prado**, **Thyssen-Bornemisza** and **Reina Sofía** museums for €30.40. It's available at the ticket desks of all three museums, allows you to visit any of the three museums at any time in the calendar year, and will save the cost of buying the three tickets separately. The ticket is valid for a one-year period from the date of purchase in the museums' ticket offices, or from the date of the selected visit upon making the purchase online.

TOP SIGHTS 17

Real Ermita de San Antonio de la Florida
Goya's "Sistine Chapel." Francisco de Goya painted the dome and vaults of this neo-Classical hermitage in 1798. After an extensive restoration, you can view this fantastic work featuring St. Anthony of Padua raising a man from the dead. Goya is buried here but not his head, which is said to have been taken by scientists who wanted to study his brain. *Info: Glorieta de San Antonio de la Florida. Tel. 915420722. Open Tue-Sun 9:30am-8pm. Closed Mon. Admission: Free. Metro: Príncipe Pío (about a 10-minute walk from the metro stop along Paseo de la Florida).*

Museo Thyssen-Bornemisza
While you can see traditional art at the Prado and contemporary art at the Reina Sofia, you can see both at the Museo Thyssen-Bornemisza. This interesting and eclectic collection (very Impressionism-heavy), acquired by the Spanish government in 1993, features works by Picasso, Velázquez, Goya, El Greco, Dürer, Caravaggio and Rembrandt. It also has a collection of contemporary works, including some by Pollock, Lichtenstein and Kandinsky, and there's an interesting section of art from the USA, including works by Georgia O'Keefe and David Hockney. On occasion, the museum showcases exhibits at the Fundación Caja Madrid at 1 Plaza San Martin, with free bus shuttle service between the two locations. *Info: 8 Paseo del Prado. Tel. 917911370. Open Tue-Sun 10am-7pm (Sat until 9pm). Admission: €13 (with English pamphlet), €9 over 65, under 18 free. Free Mon noon-4pm (permanent collection only). Metro: Banco de España. www.museothyssen.org.*

Plaza Mayor

The Plaza Mayor is an arcaded and cobblestoned square dating back to 1617. It's surrounded by buildings with balconies and is truly the heart of Viejo Madrid (Old Madrid), and one of Europe's grandest squares. Notice the colorful paintings on the Casa de la Panaderia ("bakery") on the north side of the square. It remains a meeting place for all of Madrid. That's Felipe III, who ordered this square to be built, on his horse in the center of the square. Take a stroll! *Info: Off of Calle de Mayor between Puerta del Sol and Plaza de la Villa. Metro: Sol.*

El Retiro

Behind the Prado Museum is **El Retiro**, a 350-acre park. It dates back to the 1630s, and is filled with statues, fountains, a lake, and lots of locals (and tourists) enjoying this vast green space in the midst of Madrid. Art is sometimes showcased in the **Palacio de Cristal** and the **Palacio de Velázquez**, 19th-century pavilions in the park. Also here is the **Jardín Botánico**, Madrid's large botanical garden. *Info: Botanical Garden: Open daily 10am-dusk. Admission: €6. Metro: Retiro.*

Puerta del Sol

The **Puerta del Sol** (which means "Gateway of the Sun") is always crowded. There's a bronze plaque set into the sidewalk on the south side of the square from which all distances in Spain are measured. That statue is King Charles III (who ruled from 1759-1788) on his horse. He's facing a building 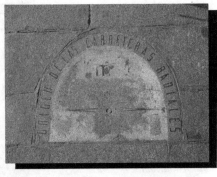 that dates back to 1768 and is now the headquarters of Madrid's regional government. Check out the huge Tio Pepe sign, Madrid's first billboard. On the corner of Calle de Carmen is a bronze statue of a bear – the symbol of Madrid. *Info: Metro: Sol.*

Convento de las Descalzas Reales

Noblewomen who entered this convent in the mid-16th century brought rich dowries. Inside you'll find an incredible collection of tapestries, a chapel with an ornate gold altar, extraordinary statues, a piece of wood said to be from Christ's cross, and paintings by the likes of Titian and Goya. *Info: 3 Plaza de las Descalzas Reales. Tel. 914548700. Open Tue-Sat 10am-2pm and 4pm-6:30pm, Sun 10am-3pm. Closed Mon. Admission: €6 (guided tours in Spanish). Some English tours in high season. Metro: Puerta del Sol. www.patrimonionacional.es.*

Museo de América
(Museum of the Americas)

Europe's best collection of pre-Columbian, Spanish-American, and Native American artifacts is found here. A few highlights are the strangest collections: shrunken heads, and sculptures of people with physical defects. *Info: 6 Avenida de los Reyes Católicos (at Avenida Arco de la Victoria next to the Faro de Madrid). Tel. 915492641. Open Tue-Sat 9:30am-3pm (Thu until 7pm), Sun 10am-3pm. Admission: €3. Closed Mon. Free Thu from 2pm. Metro: Moncloa. www.museodeamerica.mcu.es. Note that most descriptions are in Spanish only.*

Plaza de Toros de las Ventas

It's certainly not for everyone, but attending a bullfight (*corrida*) is the quintessential Spanish experience. The **Museo Taurino** (Bullfighting Museum) is also here. *Info: 237 Calle de Alcalá. Tel. 913562200 (box office). Museum open Mon-Sun 10am-6pm, during bullfight season. Metro: Ventas. For tickets, visit www.las-ventas.com.*

Plaza de la Villa

You can experience a little bit of medieval times at the Plaza de la Villa, Madrid's oldest square. It's dominated by the **Casa de la Villa**, the former town hall. Notice the two symmetrical doors. These were the entrances to the city hall and the prison, which were both located in the building. Inside are 17th-century frescoes and a stunning stained-glass ceiling. The Francisco Goya painting *La Alegoria de Madrid* depicts Madrid as a woman standing beside the municipal coat of arms. An arch connects the Casa de la Villa with the **Casa de Cisneros**, a castle which dates back to 1537. It's an example of the Plateresque style, a Spanish version of early Renaissance architecture. The 15th-century **Torre de los Lujanes** (Lujanes Tower) is one of the oldest buildings in Madrid. At the center of the square is a statue of Alvaro de Bazan, the admiral who planned the Spanish Armada's attempt to invade England. *Info: Between the Cathedral and the Plaza Mayor (off of Calle de Mayor). Metro: Ópera.*

Catedral de Nuestra Señora de la Almudena
Construction of Madrid's cathedral began in 1883 and was not completed until 1993. Admission is free, so enter through the huge sculpted doors and look up at the colorful ceiling. In a chapel behind the altar is the empty 12th-century coffin of St. Isidro, the patron saint of Madrid. Forty years after he died, the coffin was opened (now, who decided to do this?) and his body had not decayed, which was enough for the pope to canonize him. He's buried elsewhere in the city. *Info: 10 Calle de Bailén. Tel. 915592874. Open daily 9am-8:30pm. Admission: €1. Metro: Ópera. www.catedraldelaalmudena.es.*

Teatro Real
Located on the **Plaza de Oriente** (lined with statues of the kings and queens of Spain) is the **Teatro Real** (Royal Theater). It was built in 1850 and is the site of opera and ballet performances, but the real star is the interior of the building itself. Visitors can explore this elegant building, including the Royal Box. *Info: There are audio tours daily from 10:30am-4:30pm. A 50-minute tour is €7. www.teatro-real.com.*

Plaza Santa Ana

This pleasant square is located in one of Madrid's oldest neighborhoods. This is where many Madrileños congregate on weekend evenings. It's home to **Teatro Español**, the city's oldest theater dating back to 1745 and the stately Hotel Reina Victoria. There are great places to sample *tapas* in and around the square. For more information, check out the *Tapas Walk* in the *Walks* chapter of this book. *Info: To reach the square, take the metro to the Sevilla stop on Calle de Alcalá. Head south down Calle de Sevilla to the Plaza de Canalejas. Off of this plaza, head down Calle de Principe until you arrive at the Plaza Santa Ana.*

3. THE SIGHTS OF MADRID

In this chapter, we'll make your trip to **Madrid** easy by helping you plan your visit by the length of time you have and by your interests.

One Great Day in Madrid: If you have just a day in Madrid, this plan will let you experience the best the city has to offer including the Royal Palace, the Plaza Mayor, the Paseo del Arte, and an evening sampling *tapas*!

A Weekend in Fantastic Madrid: If you have a few more days in Madrid, this plan will let you experience more of the city's interesting sights.

A Wonderful Week or More in Madrid: If you have a week or more in Madrid, this plan will let you experience the best Spain's capital city has to offer. You'll also travel outside the city to experience everything from monasteries to the incredible city of Toledo.

Here are some of the day plans we have for you to enjoy!

- Churches and Religious Art
- Museum Day
- Northeast Madrid
- Northwest Madrid
- Excursions to Toledo, El Escorial Monastery & The Valley of the Fallen

A DAY IN MADRID

DON'T MISS:
Palacio Real, Madrid's Royal Palace.
Plaza Mayor, the heart of old Madrid.
Paseo del Arte, home to three fabulous art museums.
Tapas!

You're going to experience the wonderful city of Madrid with a schedule that's not too hectic or overwhelming. If you've only got a day in Madrid, you'll see some great sights like the Plaza Mayor and Palacio Real. The Prado is one the greatest–and biggest–art museums in the world, but don't try to conquer it at the expense of seeing the rest of Madrid. And a highlight (if not the highlight) of any trip to Madrid is *tapeo*, the act of bar-hopping in the early evening, eating *tapas* and drinking, before Madrid's very late dinner hour. Note that several museums are closed on Monday. All sights are shown on the A Day in Madrid Map on the next page.

Begin your day by heading to the **Puerta del Sol** ("Sol") metro stop. The Puerta del Sol (which means "Gateway of the Sun") is always crowded. That statue is King Charles III (who ruled from 1759-1788) on his horse. Check out the huge Tio Pepe sign, Madrid's first billboard. On the corner of Calle de Carmen is a bronze statue of a bear–the symbol of Madrid.

From the Puerta del Sol, head west down Calle de Arenal. On your left, look for an alleyway off of Calle del Arenal called Pasadizo de San Ginés.

Start your day with a Madrid tradition at **Chocolatería San Ginés**. This 100-year-old *chocolateria* is where you can sample *churros y porras*. *Churros* are loops and *porras* are sticks of deep-fried batter which you dip in hot chocolate. *Info: 5 Pasadizo de San Ginés (an alleyway off of Calle del Arenal). Tel. 913656546. Open daily 24 hours. Metro: Ópera or Puerta del Sol. www.chocolateriasangines.com.*

SIGHTS 25

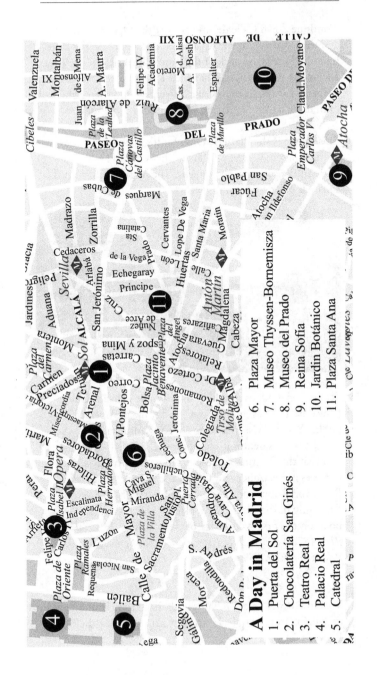

A Day in Madrid
1. Puerta del Sol
2. Chocolatería San Ginés
3. Teatro Real
4. Palacio Real
5. Catedral
6. Plaza Mayor
7. Museo Thyssen-Bornemisza
8. Museo del Prado
9. Reina Sofía
10. Jardín Botánico
11. Plaza Santa Ana

Continue down Calle de Arenal, past the Ópera metro stop and then you'll be at the square Plaza de Isabel II. The large building here is the back of the **Teatro Real** (Royal Theater). Facing the Royal Theater, head left to the street Calle de Vergara. Turn right onto Calle de Vergara and then right onto Calle de Carlos III and head into the large square.

This square is the **Plaza de Oriente**. It's lined with statues of the kings and queens of Spain (that's Philip IV on his horse in the center of the square). The huge building on the square is our destination.

Perched on a hill overlooking the city, the **Palacio Real** (Royal Palace) has 3,000 rooms, and some are open to the public. You can visit the rooms of King Alfonso XIII, who was the last resident until he abdicated in 1931. You can also visit the Painting Gallery (filled with pieces by such notables as Velázquez and Goya), the Throne Room, the Reception Room and the Royal Armoury. The elaborate Changing of the Guard takes place in the courtyard at noon on the first Wednesday of every month. *Info: Tel. 914548700. Open daily 10am-6pm (until 8pm Apr-Sep). Admission: €10, €5 ages 5-16. Metro: Ópera. www.patrimonionacional.es.*

With the Royal Palace to your back, head right down Calle de Bailén. To your right is our next stop, just past the Royal Palace.

Construction of the **Catedral de Nuestra Señora de la Almudena** began in 1883 and was not completed until 1993. Admission is free, so enter through the huge sculpted doors and look up at the colorful ceiling. *Info: 10 Calle de Bailén. Tel. 915592874. Open daily 9am-8:30pm. Admission: €1. Metro: Ópera. www.catedraldelaalmudena.es.*

Continue down Calle de Bailén until you reach Calle Mayor. Take a left onto Calle Mayor.

You can experience a little bit of medieval times at the **Plaza de la Villa**, Madrid's oldest square, dominated by the Casa de la Villa, the former town hall (to your right). The building straight ahead is Casa de Cisneros, which dates back to 1537. To your left is the 15th-century tower Torre de los Lujanes.

You'll turn right onto Cava de San Miguel from Calle Mayor and soon see the entrance to the heart of Madrid.

The **Plaza Mayor** is an arcaded and cobblestoned square dating back to 1617. It's surrounded by buildings with balconies and is truly the heart of Viejo Madrid (Old Madrid), and one of Europe's grandest squares. Notice the colorful paintings on the Casa de la Panaderia ("bakery") on the north side of the square. It remains a meeting place for all of Madrid. That's Felipe III, who ordered this square to be built, on his horse in the center of the square. Take a stroll!

You can exit the square through the northeast corner (between numbers 31 and 32) onto the street Calle de la Sal. Turn left onto Calle de Postas, and then continue on to the large square Puerta del Sol (where you began your day).

From the square, head east in the direction of the Tio Pepe sign (the street to the right of the Tio Pepe sign) on Carrera de San Jerónimo.

At the corner of Calle Victoria is the **Museo del Jamón** at 6 Carrera de San Jerónimo. The "Museum of Ham" isn't really a museum, but a chain of delis serving and selling ham. You can't miss it, as you'll see hundreds of hams hanging from the ceiling. Try a glass of sherry and cured ham. There's a restaurant upstairs (where you'll pay more).

If you want a drink or something to eat, another choice is Salon Puerta del Sol at number 16, a beautiful eatery with stone walls and ornate carved wood.

If you continue down Carrera de San Jerónimo, you'll soon find yourself at the beautiful fountain **Fuente de Neptuno** on the Plaza de Cánovas del Castillo. The fountain is named after the Roman god of the sea.

You're approaching the **Paseo del Arte**, home to three fabulous art museums: **Museo Thyssen-Bornemisza**, **Museo del Prado** and **Reina Sofía**. Although some might balk at this suggestion, if you only have a short time in Madrid,

I'd visit the **Museo Thyssen-Bornemisza**. While you can see traditional art at the Prado and contemporary art at the Reina Sofia, you can see both at this museum. The great thing about choosing between these three museums so near to each other is that you just can't go wrong with whichever one you pick. The Museo Thyssen-Bornemisza is at 8 Paseo del Prado. It contains an interesting and eclectic collection, acquired by the Spanish government in 1993, featuring works by Picasso, Velázquez, Goya, El Greco and Rembrandt. It also has a collection of contemporary works, including some by Pollock, Lichtenstein and Kandinsky. *Info: 8 Paseo del Prado. Tel. 917911370. Open Tue-Sun 10am-7pm (Sat until 9pm). Admission: €13 (with English pamphlet), €9 over 65, under 18 free. Free Mon noon-4pm (permanent collection only).Metro: Banco de España. www.museothyssen.org.*

If you head to your right down the Paseo del Prado, you'll see a massive museum on your left. The **Museo del Prado** is one of Europe's greatest museums, with 7,000 paintings by such notables as Velázquez, Goya, El Greco, Titian, Botticelli, Murillo and Rubens. *Info: Paseo del Prado. Tel. 913302880. Open: Mon-Sat 10am-8pm, Sun and holidays 10am-7pm. Closed Jan1, May 1, and Dec 25. Reduced hours Jan 6, May 1, Dec 24, and Dec 31 10am-2pm. Admission: €15. €7.50 students 18-25 and over 65. Under 18 free. Free Mon-Sat 6pm-8pm and Sun 5pm-7pm. Metro: Banco de España or Atocha. www.museodelprado.es.*

If you walk past the museum, you'll see the **Jardín Botánico**, Madrid's large botanic garden (open daily, €6). Behind the museum is **El Retiro**, a 350-acre park. It dates back to the

1630s, and is filled with statues, fountains, a lake, and lots of locals (and tourists) enjoying this vast green space in the midst of Madrid. Art is showcased in the Palacio de Cristal and the Palacio de Velázquez, 19th-century pavilions in the park.

Also nearby is the **Reina Sofía**, home to a fantastic contemporary-art collection. *Info: 52 Calle de Santa Isabel. Tel. 917741000. Open Mon and Wed-Sat 10am-9pm, Sun 10am-7pm. Closed Tue. Free Mon and Wed-Sat 7pm-9pm and Sun 1:30pm-7pm. (only a portion of the museum is open during free admission). Closed Jan 1, Jan 6, May 1, May 15, Nov 9, Dec 25 and Dec 31. Admission: €10. www. museoreinasofia.es.*

For dinner, you have to have *tapas*! Head to the **Plaza Santa Ana** (the nearest metro stop is Sevilla, then walk south down Calle Sevilla to Calle de Principe). This pleasant square is located in one of Madrid's oldest neighborhoods. This is where you'll find many *tapas* restaurants.

After dinner, head back to the **Plaza Mayor**, stroll around the square, and then stop at a café and have a glass of *vino tinto* (red wine). What a great way to end your day in Madrid!

A WEEKEND IN MADRID

DON'T MISS:
Tapas!
Palacio Real, Madrid's Royal Palace.
Plaza Mayor, the heart of old Madrid.
The **Museo Thyssen-Bornemisza**, where you can see both traditional and contemporary art.
The **Real Ermita de San Antonio de la Florida** and Goya's tomb.
Exploring the fun **Chueca** neighborhood.

If you have a weekend in Madrid, you'll see some great sights like the **Plaza Mayor** and **Palacio Real**. Of course, you'll experience *tapeo*, the act of bar-hopping in the early evening, eating *tapas* and drinking. You'll explore fun neighborhoods like **Chueca** and view some of the best art collections in the world. All sights are shown on the Madrid Major Sights Map, unless noted.

Friday Evening
For dinner, you have to have *tapas*! Head to the **Plaza Santa Ana** (the nearest metro stop is Sevilla, then walk south down Calle Sevilla to Calle de Principe). This pleasant square is located in one of Madrid's oldest neighborhoods.

This is where many Madrileños congregate on weekend evenings. It's home to Teatro Español, the city's oldest theater, dating back to 1745. Also on the square is the stately Hotel Reina Victoria.

There are great places to take a break here, especially **Cervecería Alemana** at number 6. One street off of the square (at the end of Calle de Principe) is **Casa Alberto** at 18 Calle de las Huertas. This *taberna* and restaurant has been open since 1827. You'll have great *tapas* or main courses at reasonable prices, and the staff is exceptionally friendly. *Info: 18 Calle de las Huertas (a block off of the Plaza Santa Ana). Tel. 914299356. Closed Mon and after 4pm on Sun. Metro: Sevilla.*

After dinner, head back to the **Plaza Santa Ana**, stroll around the square, and then stop at a one of the *tapas* bars here and have a glass of *vino tinto* (red wine). What a great way to end your first day in Madrid!

Saturday
Begin your day by heading to the **Puerta del Sol** ("Sol") metro stop. The Puerta del Sol (which means "Gateway of the Sun") is always crowded. There's a bronze plaque set into the sidewalk on the south side of the square from which all distances in Spain are measured. That statue is King Charles III (who ruled from 1759-1788) on his horse. He's facing a building that dates back to 1768 and is now the headquarters of Madrid's regional government. Check out the huge Tio Pepe sign, Madrid's first billboard. On the corner of Calle de Carmen is a bronze statue of a bear–the symbol of Madrid.

From the Puerta del Sol, head west down Calle de Arenal. On your left, look for an alleyway off of Calle del Arenal called Pasadizo de San Ginés.

Start your day with a Madrid tradition at **Chocolatería San Ginés**. This 100-year-old *chocolateria* is where you can sample *churros y porras*. *Churros* are loops and *porras* are sticks of deep-fried batter which you dip in hot chocolate. *Info: 5 Pasadizo de San Ginés (an alleyway off of Calle del Arenal). Tel. 913656546. Open daily 24 hours. Metro: Ópera or Puerta del Sol. www.chocolateriasangines.com.*

Continue down Calle de Arenal past the Ópera metro stop, and then you'll be at the square Plaza de Isabel II. The large building here is the back of the **Royal Theater**. Facing the Royal Theater, head left to the street Calle de Vergara. Turn right onto Calle de Vergara and then right onto Calle de Carlos III and head into the large square.

This square is the **Plaza de Oriente**. It's lined with statues of the kings and queens of Spain (that's Philip IV on his horse in the center of the square).

On one side of the square is the **Teatro Real** (Royal Theater). It was built in 1850 and is the site of opera and ballet performances, but the real star here is the interior of the building itself. *Info: There are audio tours daily from 10:30am-4:30pm. A 50-minute tour is €7. www.teatro-real.com.*

That huge building on the square is our destination. Perched on a hill overlooking the city, the **Palacio Real** (Royal Palace) has 3,000 rooms, and some are open to the public. You can visit the rooms of King Alfonso XIII, who was the last resident until he abdicated in 1931. The present building dates back to 1738, and is built on the sight of

a former Moorish fortress. You can also visit the Painting Gallery (filled with pieces by such notables as Velázquez and Goya), the Throne Room, the Reception Room and the Royal Armoury. The elaborate Changing of the Guard takes place in the courtyard at noon on the first Wednesday of every month. *Info: Tel. 914548700. Open daily 10am-6pm (until 8pm Apr-Sep). Admission: €10, €5 ages 5-16. Metro: Ópera. www.patrimonionacional.es.*

Behind the Palacio Royal (Royal Palace) is a vast green space (you must enter from the street Paseo de la Virgen del Puerto, which is quite a walk from the palace). The name of this garden, **Campo del Moro** or "Moorish Camp," comes from when the Arabs used this area as a camp during their war against the Christians prior to the 16th century. The garden is modeled after a traditional English park. There are two wonderful fountains in the park, Los Tritones (Tritons Fountain) and Las Conchas (Shell Fountain). Directly north of the Royal Palace are the Jardines de Sabatini, attractive gardens with manicured hedges.

With the Royal Palace to your back, head right down Calle de Bailén. To your right is our next stop, just past the Royal Palace.

Construction of the **Catedral de Nuestra Señora de la Almudena** began in 1883 and was not completed until 1993. Admission is free, so enter through the huge sculpted doors and look up at the colorful ceiling. *Info: 10 Calle de Bailén. Tel. 915592874. Open daily 9am-8:30pm. Admission: €1. Metro: Ópera. www.catedraldelaalmudena.es.*

Continue down Calle de Bailén until you reach Calle Mayor. Take a left onto Calle Mayor. You'll turn right onto Cava de San Miguel.

The narrow bars that look like caves here are called *mesones*, and are interesting places for late-night *sangria*. This is also a great area to have a drink and *tapas*. At number 17 is **Botín**, Madrid's oldest restaurant, made famous in Ernest Hemingway's *The Sun Also Rises*. You'll eat in tiled, wood-beamed dining rooms in Madrid's (and allegedly, the world's) oldest restaurant. It's quite touristy, but the food, especially roast suckling pig (*cochinillo assado*), won't disappoint.

You'll soon see the entrance to the heart of Madrid. The **Plaza Mayor** is an arcaded and cobblestoned square dating back to 1617. It's surrounded by buildings with balconies and is truly the heart of Viejo Madrid (Old Madrid), and one of Europe's grandest squares. Throughout the years the square has seen everything from public executions during the Inquisition to bullfights. Notice the colorful paintings on the Casa de la Panaderia ("bakery") on the north side of the square. It remains a meeting place for all of Madrid, and is the sight of frequent markets and festivals. That's Felipe III, who ordered this square to be built, on his horse in the center of the square. Take a stroll: there are plenty of places in and around the square to have a snack and a drink.

In the afternoon, head to the **Paseo del Arte** along the Paseo del Prado. This street is home to three fantastic museums.

The star is the famous **Museo del Prado**, one of Europe's greatest museums. *Info: Paseo del Prado. Tel. 913302880. Open: Mon-Sat 10am-8pm, Sun and holidays 10am-7pm. Closed Jan1, May 1, and Dec 25. Reduced hours Jan 6, May 1, Dec 24, and Dec 31 10am-2pm. Admission: €15. €7.50 students 18-25 and over 65. Under 18 free. Free Mon-Sat 6pm-8pm and Sun 5pm-7pm. Metro: Banco de España or Atocha. www.museodelprado.es.*

Also here is the **Reina Sofía**, home to a fantastic contemporary-art collection. *Info: 52 Calle de Santa Isabel. Tel. 917741000. Open Mon and Wed-Sat 10am-9pm, Sun 10am-7pm. Closed Tue. Free Mon and Wed-Sat 7pm-9pm and Sun 1:30pm-7pm. (only a portion of the museum is open during free admission). Closed Jan 1, Jan 6, May 1, May 15, Nov 9, Dec 25 and Dec 31. Admission: €10. www. museoreinasofia.es.*

Although some might balk at this suggestion, if you only have a short time in Madrid, I'd visit the **Museo Thyssen-**

Bornemisza. While you can see traditional art at the Prado and contemporary art at the Reina Sofia, you can see both at this museum. *Info: 8 Paseo del Prado. Tel. 917911370. Open Tue-Sun 10am-7pm (Sat until 9pm). Admission: €13 (with English pamphlet), €9 over 65, under 18 free. Free Mon noon-4pm (permanent collection only). Metro: Banco de España. www.museothyssen.org.*

For dinner, try a restaurant near the Plaza Mayor. **Casa Paco** serves great steaks. *Info: 11 Plaza de Puerta Cerrada. Tel. 913663166. Closed Sun and Aug. Reservations required. Metro: La Latina. Moderate-Expensive.* Or you could try local specialties at **La Taberna del Alabardero**. *Info: 6 Calle de Felipe V. Tel. 915472577. Open daily. Metro: Ópera. Tapas(€). Restaurant (€€€). www.alabarderomadrid.es.*

After dinner, a nighttime stroll through the **Plaza Mayor** is just the way to end your day. If you're up for more, why not experience a *flamenco* performance? Here are two choices:

This touristy nightclub **Corral de la Morería** with Arab décor has nightly *flamenco* dancing performances. As you would expect in this late-night city, many shows don't begin until late in the evening. *Info: 17 Calle de la Morería. Tel. 913658446. Open daily. Shows begin at 7:30pm. Admission: €50 (includes one drink). Dinner also available. www.corraldelamoreria.com. Metro: La Latina.*

Authentic *flamenco* performances without all the glitz and tourists at **Casa Patas**. *Info: 10 Calle de Cañizares. Tel. 913690496. Shows Mon-Thu at 10:30pm, Fri-Sat 8pm and 10:30pm. Admission: €40 (includes one drink). www.casapatas.com. Metro: Antón Martín.*

Sunday
Head to the **Real Ermita de San Antonio de la Florida.** Francisco de Goya painted the dome and vaults of this neo-Classical hermitage in 1798. After an extensive restoration, you can view this fantastic work featuring St. Anthony of Padua raising a man from the dead. *Info: Glorieta de San Antonio de la Florida. Tel. 915420722. Open Tue-Sun 9:30am-8pm. Closed Mon. Admission: Free. Metro: Príncipe Pío (about a 10-minute walk from the metro stop along Paseo de la Florida). See the Northwest Map on page 55.*

For lunch, head across the street from Goya's tomb and have lunch at **Casa Mingo**. You'll share sausages, roast chicken and salad at long tables with other diners at this *bodega* (tavern). Don't leave without tasting the cider (*sidra*)! *Info: 34 Paseo de la Florida (across the street from Goya's tomb). Tel. 915477918. Open daily 11am-midnight. No reservations. No credit cards. Metro: Príncipe Pío (about a 10-minute walk from the metro stop). www.casamingo.es.*

After lunch, I suppose you could go to one of the museums you've missed, but I suggest you head to the **Chueca** neighborhood (Metro Chueca). Stroll around and experience one of Madrid's great neighborhoods.

Remember dinner is extremely late in Madrid, so before dinner head to the **Plaza de Chueca**. It's one of the best places in Madrid to people-watch. Take a look at the beautifully decorated 1897 bar **Bodega de Ángel Sierra** on the square. It's the one with the fun and diverse crowd spilling onto the square.

A WEEK IN AND AROUND MADRID

DON'T MISS:
Extraordinary religious art at the
Convento de las Descalzas Reales.
The paintings of Velázquez, Goya, and El Greco at the
Prado Museum.
Great shopping in the **Salamanca** district.
The **Real Ermita de San Antonio de la Florida** and Goya's tomb.
The amazingly preserved city of **Toledo**.

If you have a week in Madrid and the surrounding area, this plan will let you experience the best Madrid has to offer, and also take you outside the city to experience everything from monasteries to the delights of the ancient city of Toledo!

CHURCHES AND RELIGIOUS ART

Today you'll spend time visiting churches, both large and small, and see some of the best collections of religious art and artifacts in Europe. Note that many sights are closed on Monday. See the Churches/Religious Art Map on the next page.

Start your day at the Puerta del Sol (which means "Gateway of the Sun").

From the Puerta del Sol, head west down Calle de Arenal. Turn right on Calle Maestro or Calle San Martin and you will reach the Plaza de las Descalzas Reales.

Noblewomen who entered the convent **Convento de las Descalzas Reales** in the mid-16th century brought incredibly rich dowries. It isn't much to look at from the outside,

SIGHTS 39

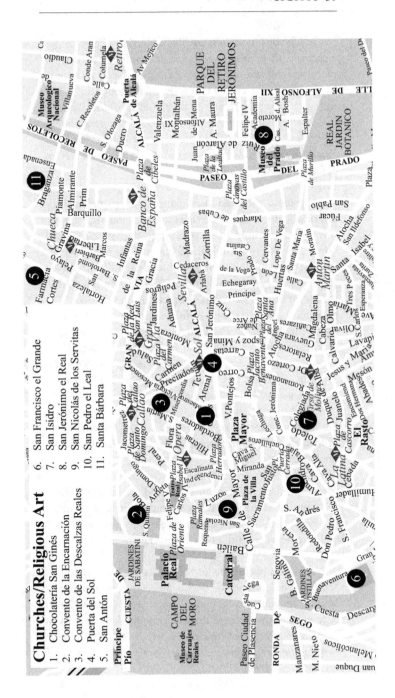

Churches/Religious Art

1. Chocolatería San Ginés
2. Convento de la Encarnación
3. Convento de las Descalzas Reales
4. Puerta del Sol
5. San Antón
6. San Francisco el Grande
7. San Isidro
8. San Jerónimo el Real
9. San Nicolás de los Servitas
10. San Pedro el Leal
11. Santa Bárbara

but inside you'll find an incredible collection of tapestries, a chapel with an ornate gold altar, extraordinary statues, a piece of wood said to be from Christ's cross, and paintings by the likes of Titian and Goya. By guided tour only (45 minutes, in Spanish). *Info: 3 Plaza de las Descalzas Reales. Tel. 914548700. Open Tue-Sat 10am-2pm and 4pm-6:30pm, Sun 10am-3pm. Closed Mon. Admission: €6 (guided tours in Spanish). Some English tours in high season. Metro: Puerta del Sol. www.patrimonionacional.es.*

If you're more interested in religious reliquaries rather than art, nearby is the **Convento de la Encarnación**. The star of this convent, built in 1611, is its reliquary that holds sacred bones and vials containing dried blood of the holy. It's said that the vial containing the dried blood of St. Pantaleón (whoever the hell that is) liquefies every year on July 27th, the anniversary of his death. Frequent medieval-music concerts are held in the beautiful and ornate chapel. The convent is located on a quiet tree-shaded square where locals play with their dogs. *Info: 1 Plaza de la Encarnación. Tel. 914548700. Open Tue-Sat 10am-2pm and 4pm-6:30pm, Fri 10:30am-12:45pm, Sun 10am-3pm. Admission: €6. Metro: Ópera. www.patrimonionacional.es.*

For lunch, try one of the restaurants, *tapas* bars, markets, or food stores listed in *Chapter 5: Sleeping & Eating* of this book.

After lunch, you'll visit some of Madrid's famous churches. You can visit as many or as few as you like, as each church won't take you long to visit. First we'll visit those religious buildings located south of the Plaza Mayor.

The small **San Nicolás de los Servitas** is Madrid's oldest. Most of it dates back to the 15th and 16th centuries, but Muslim craftsmen living under Christian rule in the 12th century built the tower in the Moorish style known as "Mudéjar." *Info: Plaza San Nicolás. Tel. 915594064. Hours open vary, but usually 10am-2pm and 6:30pm-8:30pm. Admission: Free. Metro: Ópera.*

The huge **San Francisco el Grande** with its spectacular dome was built in 1760 on the site of a Franciscan convent. Notice its seven carved walnut doors. Inside are 16th-century Gothic choir stalls, and the chapel to the left of the main entrance has an early painting by Goya of San Bernardino. *Info: Plaza de San Francisco. Tel. 913653800. Open daily. Museum: Open Tue-Sat 10:30am-12:30pm and 4pm-6pm. Admission: €5. Metro: La Latina.*

No, you didn't have too much to drink for lunch (or maybe you did). The tower of **San Pedro el Leal** is slightly leaning. Muslim craftsmen living under Christian rule in the 14th century built the tower. This is Madrid's second-oldest church (San Nicolás de los Servitas near the Plaza de Oriente is the oldest). *Info: 14 Calle Nuncio/Costanilla de San Pedro. Tel. 913651284. Usually open daily 6pm-8pm. Admission: Free. Metro: La Latina.*

The **San Isidro** basilica (also known as **La Colegiata**) was once part of a college run by the Jesuits. Built in the 17th century, it's modeled after the Gesù church in Rome. It has a beautiful, ornate altar. The remains of Madrid's patron saint, after which the basilica takes its name, are here. It's said that 40 years after his death his coffin was opened (who decided to do this?) and his body had not yet decayed. This apparently was enough to convince the then pope to canonize him. The empty coffin is at the cathedral. Notice the elaborately clothed statues in the side chapels. *Info: 37 Calle de Toledo. Tel. 913692037. Open Mon-Sun 7:30am-1pm and 6pm-9pm. Admission: Free. Metro: La Latina or Tirso de Molina.*

Across town, behind the Prado, is **San Jerónimo el Real**. Only make the trip here if you just haven't had enough churches. This Gothic church with interesting stained-glass windows is the royal church used for official ceremonies by the Spanish monarchy. *Info: 4 Calle de Moreto. Tel. 914203078. Open daily mid-Sep to Jun 10am-1pm and 5pm-8pm, Jul to mid-Sep 10am-1pm and 6pm-8:30pm. Admission: Free. Metro: Atocha.*

North of the Plaza Mayor are two churches that you can visit only if you happen to be in the neighborhood.

Construction began on the Baroque **Santa Bárbara** in 1750. Fernando VI built it for his wife Bárbara, and both are buried here. It has an extravagant interior. Above the altar is a painting of *The Visitation* (the pregnant Virgin Mary visiting her cousin Elizabeth) by Francesc de Mora. *Info: 2 Calle del General Castaños (at Calle de Bárbara de Braganza). No phone. Open daily 11am-1pm and 6:30pm-8pm. Admission: Free. Metro: Alonso Martínez.*

San Antón is named after St. Anthony of Egypt, who is said to have been good with animals (just like St. Francis). Coincidentally, what is said to be the skull of St. Francis is on display in a wooden box in the reliquary (along with lots of other bone fragments of lesser-known saints). If you come here on St. Anthony's feast day (January 17th), you'll see farm animals and pets with their owners lined up for the blessing of the animals. *Info: 63 Calle de Hortaleza (at the corner of Calle de la Farmacia). Tel. 915215781. Open Sun for masses only. Metro: Chueca.*

For dinner, try one of these great restaurants south of the Plaza Mayor (Metro: La Latina):

Casa Lucio serves Spanish cuisine in an attractive setting (tiled floors, exposed brick walls and hams hanging from the ceiling). A specialty at this popular restaurant is *churrasco* (thick grilled steak). *Info: 35 Cava Baja. Tel. 913653252. Closed Aug. Metro: La Latina. www.casalucio.es.*

At **Casa Paco** you order steaks by weight in the tiled dining rooms. Grilled lamb and fish are also served. *Info: 11 Plaza de Puerta Cerrada. Tel. 913663167. Closed Sun and Aug. Reservations required. Metro: La Latina. www.casapaco1933.es.*

After dinner, a nighttime stroll through the **Plaza Mayor** is just the way to end your day. You'll be within walking distance of both restaurants.

MUSEUM DAY

Madrid is a great city for visiting museums, and today we'll visit the Paseo del Arte (Metro: Atocha or Banco de España).

Three fantastic museums along the street Paseo del Prado make Madrid a great destination for lovers of world-class art.

The **Paseo del Arte** ticket allows entry to the **Prado**, **Thyssen-Bornemisza** and **Reina Sofía** museums for €30.40. It's available at the ticket desks of all three museums, allows you to visit any of the three museums at any time in the calendar year, and will save the cost of buying the three tickets separately. The ticket is valid for a one-year period from the date of purchase in the museums' ticket offices, or from the date of the selected visit upon making the purchase online.

If you travel to Madrid to see traditional art, you head for the Prado. If you're interested in 20th-century art, come to the **Museo Nacional Centro de Arte Reina Sofía**. This contemporary-art museum is housed in an 18th-century building that once was a hospital. There is an emphasis on 20th-century Spanish artists such as Picasso, Miró and Dalí. It's most famous painting is Picasso's masterpiece, *Guernica*, an anti-war painting of the bombing of the town of

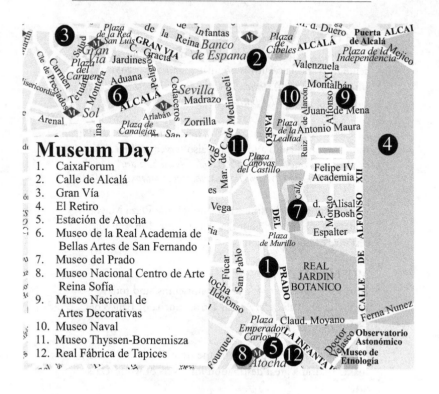

Museum Day
1. CaixaForum
2. Calle de Alcalá
3. Gran Vía
4. El Retiro
5. Estación de Atocha
6. Museo de la Real Academia de Bellas Artes de San Fernando
7. Museo del Prado
8. Museo Nacional Centro de Arte Reina Sofía
9. Museo Nacional de Artes Decorativas
10. Museo Naval
11. Museo Thyssen-Bornemisza
12. Real Fábrica de Tapices

Guernica by the Germans during the Spanish Civil War. The museum recently opened a spectacular new wing, and there are great views from the transparent exterior elevators. *Info: 52 Calle de Santa Isabel. Tel. 917741000. Open Mon and Wed-Sat 10am-9pm, Sun 10am-7pm. Closed Tue. Free Mon and Wed-Sat 7pm-9pm and Sun 1:30pm-7pm. (only a portion of the museum is open during free admission). Closed Jan 1, Jan 6, May 1, May 15, Nov 9, Dec 25 and Dec 31. Admission: €10. www. museoreinasofia.es.*

While you can see traditional art at the Prado and contemporary art at the Reina Sofía, you can see both at the **Museo Thyssen-Bornemisza**. This interesting and eclectic collection (very Impressionism-heavy), acquired by the Spanish government in 1993, features works by Picasso, Velázquez, Goya, El Greco, Dürer, Caravaggio and Rembrandt. It also has a collection of contemporary works, including some by Pollock, Lichtenstein and Kandinsky, and there's an interesting section of art from the USA, including works by Georgia O'Keefe and David Hockney. On occasion, the museum showcases exhibits at the Fundación Caja Madrid at 1 Plaza San Martin, with free bus shuttle service between the two locations. *Info: 8 Paseo del Prado. Tel. 917911370. Open Tue-Sun 10am-7pm (Sat until 9pm). Admission: €13 (with English pamphlet), €9 over 65, under 18 free. Free Mon noon-4pm (permanent collection only).Metro: Banco de España. www.museothyssen.org.*

The **Museo del Prado** (Prado Museum) is one of Europe's greatest museums, with 7,000 paintings (1,500 are on display at any one time) by such biggies as Velázquez, Goya, El Greco, Titian, Botticelli, Murillo and Rubens. A few Prado highlights are:

Garden of Love by Rubens
Immaculate Conception by Murillo
Third of May by Goya
Christ Carrying the Cross by El Greco
The Maids of Honor (Las Meninas) by Velázquez
David and Goliath by Caravaggio
Martyrdom of St. Philip by Ribera
The Annunciation by Fra Angélico
Phillip II by Titian
The Hay Cart by Bosch
St. Peter Crucified Appearing to Peter Nolasco by Zurbarán
Adam and Eve by Dürer

For many, the most stunning paintings here are Goya's late-life dark and disturbing Black Paintings, especially *Saturn Devouring One of His Sons*.

Info: Paseo del Prado. Tel. 913302880. Open: Mon-Sat 10am-8pm, Sun and holidays 10am-7pm. Closed Jan 1, May 1, and Dec 25. Reduced hours Jan 6, May 1, Dec 24, and Dec 31 10am-2pm. Admission: €15. €7.50 students 18-25 and over 65. Under 18 free. Free Mon-Sat 6pm-8pm and Sun 5pm-7pm. Metro: Banco de España or Atocha. www.museodelprado.es.

Had enough art? Head to **El Retiro**. This 350-acre park behind the Prado dates back to the 1630s, and is filled with statues, fountains, a lake, and lots of locals (and tourists) enjoying this vast green space in the midst of Madrid. The huge Monument of Alfonso XII, built in 1901, faces the boating lake. In the heart of the park sitting next to a small lake is the Palacio de Cristal (Crystal Palace). This wrought iron-and-glass domed building dates back to the 1880s, and is frequently the site of contemporary-art exhibitions. One oddity here is in the southern end of the park at the intersection of Paseo del Uruguay and Paseo del Cuba. The Angel Caído (Fallen Angel) is said to be the world's only public monument (and fountain) dedicated to the devil. Lucifer is shown as a handsome young "devil" seemingly wrestling with a snake. Below are demons clutching alligators. See photo below. At the southwest corner of the park is the **Jardin Botánico**, a large botanic garden (open daily from 10am to dusk, €6). *Info: Entrance at Calle de Alfonso XII. Metro: Banco de España, Atocha or Retiro.*

El Retiro is a huge park. If you'd rather not walk around in the park or just don't have much time, head to a nearby railway station. Why would you want to do that? The **Estación de Atocha** is at Plaza del Emperador Carlos V at the southern end of Paseo del Prado (Metro: Atocha). The grand iron-and-glass Atocha Railway Station is worth a visit even if you're not hopping on the AVE, Spain's high-speed trains. It's a masterpiece of 19th-century railway architecture. What makes it even more interesting is the fantastic **tropical garden** located inside.

Not too far from the Paseo del Prado are several other museums that you may want to visit depending on your interests. These are lesser-known museums you should try to visit only after you've seen the big three art museums listed above:

Columbus and other explorers brought back lots of stuff to Spain, and the **Museo Naval** (Navy Museum) is loaded with everything from primitive weapons to the first known map of the Americas. A huge wall map traces the routes of Spanish mariners. *Info: 5 Paseo del Prado. Tel. 915238789. Open Tue-Sun 10am-7pm. Closed Mon. Admission: Free. Metro: Banco de España. www.armada.mde.es.*

Located in a 17th-century Baroque palace (not too far from the Puerta del Sol), Madrid's Fine Arts Museum **Museo de la Real Academia de Bellas Artes de San Fernando** features paintings and sculptures from the 16th century to today. You'll see works by Goya (including two self-portraits), El Greco, Murillo, Rubens and Velázquez, to name a few. Nearby at 48 Calle de Alcalá is the **Círculo de Bellas Artes** (Fine Arts Circle), a cultural center hosting changing exhibits and activities. It has a beautiful café overlooking Calle de Alcalá. *Info: 13 Calle de Alcalá. Tel. 915240864. Open Tue-Sun 10am-3pm. Closed Mon. Admission: €8. Free Wed. Metro: Puerta del Sol or Sevilla. www.realacademiabellasartes-sanfernando.com.*

A huge collection of decorative pieces, furniture and ceramics is found in the **Museo Nacional de Artes Decorativas**, including everything from crucifixes to tapestries. There's also an elaborately tiled, 18th-century kitchen featuring period household goods. *Info: 12 Calle de Montalbán. Open Tue-Sat 9:30am-3pm, Sun 10am-3pm. Tel. 915326499. Admission: €3. Free Sun. Metro: Banco de España. mnartes-decorativas.mcu.es.*

The **Real Fábrica de Tapices** (Royal Tapestry Factory) opened in 1721, and not much has changed since 1889 when it moved to this location. You can watch traditional tapestry making, many based on designs by Goya. Frankly, the tour didn't do much for me. *Info: 2 Calle de Fuenterrabía. Tel. 914340550. Open Mon-Fri 10am-2pm (one-hour guided tours only. English tours Mon-Fri at 12:30pm). Admission: €5. Metro: Menéndez Pelayo. www.realfatapices.com.*

Calle de Alcalá is one of Madrid's grandest streets. (Metro: Puerta del Sol, Sevilla, Banco de España and Retiro). This street has several important sights. At Plaza de Cibeles is the post-office building (referred to as both the **Palacio de Comunicaciones** or **Correos**) that looks like a massive wedding cake. It houses a small museum (Museo Postal y Telegráfico) with a large collection of rare stamps and exhibits on the history of communication. Across from the post office is the grand **Banco de España** (Bank of Spain) building. Also here is the late 19th-century palace, **Palacio de Linares**, home to the Casa de América, a Latin American cultural center with changing exhibits (the one with the flags of the U.S. and Latin American countries in front of it). The marble fountain in the square features **La Cibeles**, a fertility goddess, sitting in a chariot drawn by two lions.

On the northern end of the square is the **Palacio Buenavista**, which is the headquarters of the Spanish Army. One of the many impressive buildings on this street is the **Edificio Metrópolis** at number 39. It was built in 1911 and features statues representing trade, industry, agriculture and mining.

At Plaza de la Independencia is the **Puerta de Alcalá**, the great city gate (impressively lit at night).

And if you're up to more exploring, the **Gran Vía** intersects with the Calle de Alcalá. This broad boulevard (the name means "Grand Way") was created in 1910. At its western end is the **Plaza de España**, which is dominated by fascist-type architecture erected in the early 1950s. In the center of the square are statues of Don Quixote, Cervantes and Sancho Panza. Grand buildings, mostly housing financial institutions, line the boulevard. Check out the ornamental neo-Classical **Edificio la Estrella** at number 10, and the 1920s Manhattan-style **Telefónica** building at number 28.

A DAY IN NORTHEAST MADRID

Today you'll explore the interesting neighborhoods of Chueca, Salamanca and Retiro. We'll visit two less-frequented museums and stroll through these interesting neighborhoods. Note that both the Sorolla Museum and the Lázaro Galdiano Museum are closed on Monday. See the Northeast map on the next page.

Start your day by taking the metro to the Rubén Darío stop. Within walking distance of this stop are two museums, both small enough that you could visit them in a relatively short time. If you're interested in art, head to the **Museo Sorolla**. Joaquín Sorolla is known as Spain's leading Impressionist painter; he was actually a student of "luminism," the study of the effects of light on objects. The subjects of his paintings are mainly the sun-drenched places of his native Valencia. His works are housed here (his former home built in 1910) along with a collection of his personal effects. The meticulously maintained gardens were designed by Sorolla and contain a collection of attractive fountains. *Info: 37 Paseo de General Martínez Campos (at the corner of Calle de Zurbano). Tel. 913101584. Open Tue-Sat 9:30 am-8pm, Sun 10am-3pm. Admission: €3. Free Sun. Metro: Rubén Darío, Iglesia, or Gregorio Marañón. museosorolla. mcu.es.*

If you have time, head next to the **Museo Lázaro Galdiano**. Galdiano (who died in 1948) was a banker, collector of art, and an avid traveler. One step into the grand Central Hall with its richly decorated doorways and you'll immediately know what you're in for. His diverse collection of 15,000 items, housed in a lavish palace, includes everything from household goods to medieval stained glass to paintings by Rembrandt, El Greco, Goya, Murillo, and other important artists. There's also a stunning collection of 7th- to 19th-century jewelry. *Info: 122 Calle de Serrano (at Calle de María de Molina). Tel. 915616084. Open Tue-Sat 10am-4:30pm, Sun 10am-3pm. Closed Mon. Admission: €7. Metro: Rubén Darío or Núñez de Balboa. www.museolazarogaldiano.es.*

SIGHTS 51

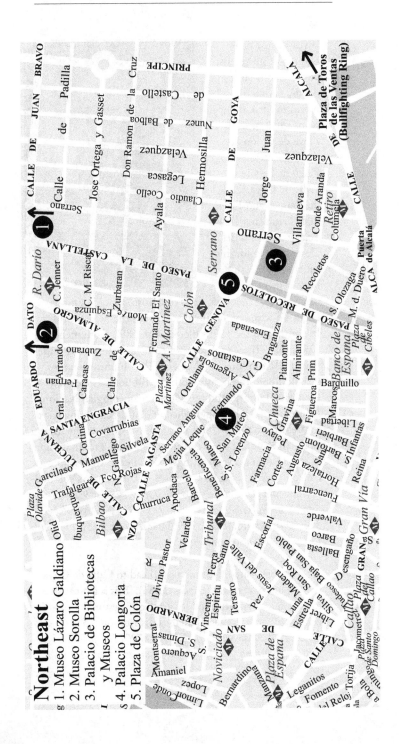

Northeast
1. Museo Lázaro Galdiano
2. Museo Sorolla
3. Palacio de Bibliotecas y Museos
4. Palacio Longoria
5. Plaza de Colón

If you've just had enough of museums, you can start your day by taking the metro to the Colón stop. You'll be at the **Plaza de Colón** (at the intersection of Paseo de Recoletos, Calle de Goya, Calle de Génova and Paseo de la Castellana). Officially the Plaza del Descubrimiento, this square features three huge cement blocks  (representing the three ships of Christopher Columbus) engraved with text on the discovery of the New World. In contrast to the 1970s blocks is an 1892 monument to Columbus. There are plenty of cafés here. Also here is the **Palacio de Bibliotecas y Museos**. This impressive neo-Classical building houses both the **Biblioteca Nacional** (National Library) and the **Museo Arqueológico Nacional** (Museum of Archeology), filled with artifacts dating back to prehistoric times. There's a primitive stone statue from 4 B.C., an elaborate 14th-century choir stall, a reproduction of the Altamira cave paintings, and an extensive Islamic collection. The main attractions date from Spain's colonial period. *Info: 13 Calle de Serrano. Open Tue-Sat 9:30am-8pm, Sun 9:30am-2:30pm. Tel. 915777912. (Archeology Museum). Admission: €3. Free Sat after 2pm and Sun. Metro: Colón or Serrano. man.mcu.es.*

After you've visited the museums, head to **Calle de Goya** (which intersects the Plaza de Colón). This is a great street for shopping. Some shops are located in restored 19th-century palaces in the **Salamanca** district. *Info: 6-8 Calle de Goya (at Calle de Serrano). Tel. 915770012. Open Mon-Sat 9:30am-9:30pm. www.jardindeserrano.es. Metro: Serrano.*

Head to the **Chueca** neighborhood (bounded on the south by the Gran Vía, on the west by Calle de Fuencarral, and on the east by the Paseo de Recoletas). Metro: Chueca.

This trendy area is home to many cafés, shops and restaurants. A seat at a café on the **Plaza de Chueca** is one of the best places in Madrid to people-watch. Take a look at the beautifully decorated 1897 bar **Bodega de Ángel Sierra** on the square. It's the one with the fun and diverse crowd spilling onto the square.

While walking around, if you happen to be around Calle de Fernando VI (don't make a special trip), you'll see, at number 4, the **Palacio Longoria**. You'll wonder if you're in Barcelona. This fantastic building, constructed in the early 1900s, is the sole Catalan Art Nouveau building in Madrid (just like all those fantastic buildings in Barcelona). It sort of looks like a sand sculpture.

An association of Spanish writers and artists owns this building, and it's not open to the public.

But you're not here to look at buildings, you're here to pop into the diverse and interesting shops and people-watch.

There's plenty of nightlife in the Chueca neighborhood. Be prepared to stay up late!

THE DIVERSE SIGHTS OF NORTHWEST MADRID
Note that most sights on this day are closed on Monday. See the Northwest map on the next page.

In the morning, head to the **Real Ermita de San Antonio de la Florida**, Goya's "Sistine Chapel." Francisco de Goya painted the dome and vaults of this neo-Classical hermitage in 1798. After an extensive restoration, you can view this fantastic work featuring St. Anthony of Padua raising a man from the dead. Goya is buried here but not his head, which is said to have been taken by scientists who wanted to study his brain. *Info: Glorieta de San Antonio de la Florida. Tel. 915420722. Open Tue-Sun 9:30am-8pm. Closed Mon. Admission: Free. Metro: Príncipe Pío (about a 10-minute walk from the metro stop along Paseo de la Florida).*

For lunch, head across the street from Goya's tomb and have lunch at **Casa Mingo**. You'll share sausages, roast chicken and salad at long tables with other diners at this *bodega* (tavern). Don't leave without tasting the cider (*sidra*)! *Info: 34 Paseo de la Florida (across the street from Goya's tomb). Tel. 915477918. Open daily 11am-midnight. No reservations. No credit cards. Metro: Príncipe Pío (about a 10-minute walk from the metro stop). www.casamingo.es.*

After lunch, you have several choices (depending on your interests).

SIGHTS 55

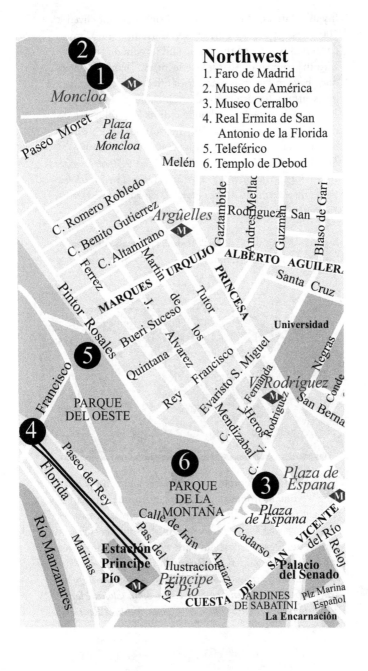

Northwest
1. Faro de Madrid
2. Museo de América
3. Museo Cerralbo
4. Real Ermita de San Antonio de la Florida
5. Teleférico
6. Templo de Debod

If you're interested in seeing how Spanish nobility lived 100 years ago, head to the **Museo Cerralbo**. The Marquis de Cerralbo donated this house and its contents to the city with the stipulation that it be left intact. Thank God you don't have to dust this place! It's stuffed with clocks, marble busts, armor, furnishings and art, including El Greco's *Ecstasy of St. Francis*. The house with its incredibly ornate rooms is the real star, especially the sumptuous mirrored ballroom and the grand staircase. *Info: 17 Calle de Ventura Rodríguez. Tel. 915473646. Open Tue-Sat 9:30am-3pm, Sun 10am-3pm. Admission: €3. Free Sun. Open Thu 5pm-8pm with Free Admission. Metro: Plaza de España. www.culturaydeporte.gob.es/mcerralbo.*

If you don't want to be stuck inside, go across the street from the Museo Cerralbo.

The 4th-century **Templo de Debod** was a gift to the Spanish government from the Egyptian government in thanks for Spain's assistance in helping to save Egyptian treasures from the Aswan Dam. It's located in the south corner of the **Parque del Oeste**, a peaceful park with statues, fountains, and a huge rose garden (**La Rosaleda**). *Info: Paseo del Pintor Rosales (near the intersection of Calle de Ventura Rodríguez). Tel. 913667415. Open Tue-Sun 10am-8pm. Closed Mon. Admission: Free. Metro: Plaza de España, Ventura Rodríguez or Argüelles.*

Also in the park is the **Teleférico**. This cable car's destination is an amusement park (**Parque de Atracciones**), zoo and aquarium. It's a great way to see all of Madrid. One-way trip (1.5 miles) takes eleven minutes. *Info: Paseo del Pintor Rosales at the east edge of Parque del Oeste (near the corner of Calle del Marqués de Urquijo). Tel. 915411118. Hours change frequently, so consult teleferico.emtmadrid. es. Admission: €6 round-trip. Metro: Plaza de España or Argüelles.*

If you're interested in the history of the Americas, visit the **Museo de América** (Museum of the Americas). Europe's best collection of pre-Columbian, Spanish-American, and Native American artifacts is found here. Most date from the time of the Spanish conquest of Central and South America. A few highlights are the strangest collections: shrunken heads, and sculptures of people with physical defects. *Info: 6 Avenida de los Reyes Católicos (at Avenida Arco de la Victoria next to the Faro de Madrid). Tel. 915492641. Open Tue-Sat 9:30am-3pm (Thu until 7pm), Sun 10am-3pm. Admission: €3. Closed Mon. Free Thu from 2pm. Metro: Moncloa. www.museodeamerica.mcu.es. Note that most descriptions are in Spanish only.*

Next to the Museo de América is the **Faro de Madrid**. This observation tower (it sort of looks like the Seattle Space Needle) offers a quick glass-walled elevator ride up for great views. *Info: Avenida de los Reyes Católicos (at the west end of Calle de la Princesa). Tel. 915501251. Open Tue-Sun 9:30am-7:30pm. Admission: €3. Metro:*

That white arch nearby is the **Arco de la Victoria**, erected by dictator Francisco Franco in 1956 to celebrate the Nationalist victory in the Spanish Civil War (1936-39).

Finally, if you're interested in fashion, head to the **Museo del Traje** (Museum of Clothing). A collection of historic clothing is housed in this museum located in a modern facility that opened in 2004. One popular exhibit shows fashion in film, featuring such movies as Casablanca and Funny Face. There's also an interesting museum shop and a cafeteria here. *Info: 2 Avenida de Juan de Herrera. Tel. 915504700. Open Tue-Sat 9:30am-7pm, Sun 10am-3pm. Open Thu Jul-Aug until 10:30pm. Closed Mon. Admission: €3. Free Sat after 2:30pm and Sun. Metro: Moncloa. museodeltraje.mcu. es. Note that the permanent collection is closed for renovations until later in 2020. Temporary exhibitions are open.*

TOLEDO

Just a short distance (44 miles [71 km]) from Madrid, the amazingly preserved city of Toledo, perched on a rocky mound, is the historic center of Spain. From the 11th to the 13th centuries, Toledo was a city of three cultures, as Christian, Jewish and Muslim communities coexisted and flourished. Travelers will find this fascinating mix appealing. Yes, there are throngs of tourists, especially during the summer high season, but try to spend the night, when Toledo's narrow medieval streets come to life filled with locals. Another benefit of an overnight stay is that the city is lit by floodlights, making it look extraordinary. You'll find Jewish synagogues, an incredible cathedral and famous art, especially works by Toledo's famous former resident: El Greco. All of Toledo's sights are within walking distance of each other.

By bus, Toledo is an hour and 15 minutes from Madrid. Two buses depart each hour from Plaza Eliptica in south Madrid, roundtrip fare €10, and there are several trains departing from the Atocha station in Madrid each day. A high-speed AVE train shortens the trip to 35 minutes (from €9). Book in advance at www.renfe.es/ave. It's a 15-minute walk from the bus station and a 20-minute walk from the train station to Plaza Zocódover. You can enter the city through the Puerta de Bisagra (Bisagra Gate). If arriving by car, take A-42 South or AP-41 (toll).

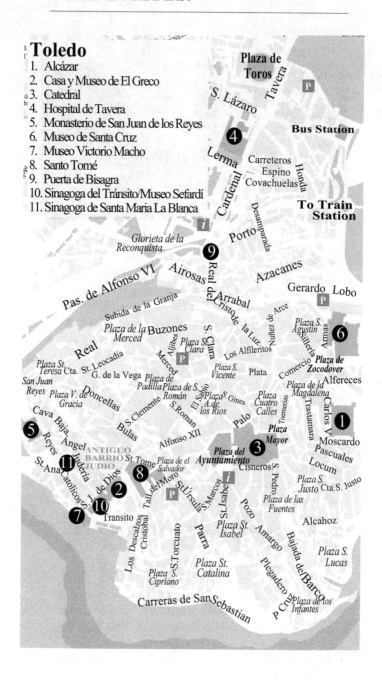

Toledo
1. Alcázar
2. Casa y Museo de El Greco
3. Catedral
4. Hospital de Tavera
5. Monasterio de San Juan de los Reyes
6. Museo de Santa Cruz
7. Museo Victorio Macho
8. Santo Tomé
9. Puerta de Bisagra
10. Sinagoga del Tránsito/Museo Sefardí
11. Sinagoga de Santa Maria La Blanca

A colorful outdoor flea market is held every Tuesday from 9am to 2pm at Bisagra Gate.

The **Antiguo Barrio Judío** (Old Jewish Quarter) is an interesting maze of narrow streets that's a great place to wander. Before the expulsion of Jews from Spain in 1492, this area was home to a vibrant Jewish community. Several important sights (listed below) remain. *Info: Southwestern edge of the old town.*

There are several sights here, all within blocks of each other:

The **Casa y Museo de El Greco** is El Greco's House and Museum. El Greco (1541-1614) was a painter, sculptor and architect who was born in Crete and settled in Spain. He's regarded as the first great genius of the Spanish School. He was known as El Greco (the Greek), but his real name was Domenikos Theotocopoulos. He lived in many different apartments throughout the city. This house (he may have actually never lived here) is furnished with period pieces, and the studio is home to several of his later works. *Info: Paseo Tránsito (Old Jewish Quarter). Tel. 925990982. Open Mar-Oct Tue-Sun 9:30pm-7:30pm, Nov-Feb Tue-Sun 9:30am-6:30pm. Closed Mon. Admission: €3. Free under 18 and over 65.*

The small 14th-century chapel **Santo Tomé** is home to El Greco's 1586 masterpiece, *The Burial of the Count of Orgaz*. This large painting shows the count being lowered into his tomb by Saints Augustine and Stephen, but it's the onlookers in the painting that make this work fascinating. Notice the man looking at you (seventh figure from the left). It's said to be El Greco himself. *Info: 4 Plaza del Conde (Old Jewish Quarter). Tel. 925256098. Open daily Mar to mid-Oct 10am-6:45pm, mid-Oct to Feb 10am-5:45pm. Admission: €3. www.toledomonumental.com/santo-tome.*

The 14th-century synagogue **Sinagoga del Tránsito** has been meticulously restored, and features an elegant wooden ceiling, richly decorative arches, Moorish columns, and beautiful friezes with Hebrew inscriptions. The **Museo Sefardí** includes artifacts covering ten centuries of Sephardic history. The patio has ancient Jewish gravestones dating back to before the Jewish expulsion from Spain in 1492. *Info: Calle Samuel Leví (Jewish Quarter). Tel. 925223665. Open Tue-Sat 9:30am-6pm, Sun 10am-3pm. Closed Mon. Admission: €3.*

The **Sinagoga de Santa María la Blanca** dates back to the 12th century, and is an interesting mix of styles. It was converted to a Catholic church in the early 15th century. Moorish horseshoe arches make the place look a bit like a mosque. *Info: 2-4 Calle de los Reyes Católicos. Tel. 925227257. Open daily Oct-Mar 10am-5:45pm, Apr-Sep 10am-6:45pm. Admission: €2.*

The grand Gothic-Spanish-Flemish **Monasterio de San Juan de los Reyes** (Monastery of St. John of the Kings) was commissioned by King Ferdinand and Queen Isabella in 1476 to celebrate their victory over the Portuguese. The interior features sculptures of liberated Catholic slaves. If you visit, don't miss the lovely cloisters. *Info: 17 Calle Reyes Católicos. Tel. 925227257. Open daily mid-Oct to Feb 10am-5:45pm, Mar to mid-Oct 10am-6:45pm. Admission: €3.*

The former home and workshop of Victorio Macho, an early-20th-century sculptor, is now the **Museo Victorio Macho** (Victorio Macho Museum) dedicated to his work. It overlooks the gorge providing interesting views of Toledo. Also here is an air-conditioned theater featuring a 10-minute video of Toledo's history (with showings in English). *Info: 2 Plaza de Victorio Macho. Tel. 925284225. Open Mon-Sat 10am-7pm, Sun 10am-3pm. Admission: €3.*

SIGHTS 63

Now head to the **Alcázar**. You can't miss this huge fortress looming over the city. In 1936, during the Spanish Civil War, it was almost destroyed during a 70-day siege. It's been rebuilt and now houses a military museum. It's on the Plaza de Zocódover where all of Toledo seems to congregate in the early evening. *Info: Calle General Moscardó and Cuesta de Carlos V. Tel. 925238800. Open Tue-Sun 10am-5pm. Closed Mon. Admission: €5.*

It took almost three centuries (1226-1493) to build the **Catedral**, a Gothic masterpiece. It's Spain's second-largest (the one in Seville is larger), and has 750 stained-glass windows. Notice the red cardinals' hats hanging from the ceiling over the spots where they're buried. Legend has it that when the hat falls from the ceiling, that particular cardinal's soul is released from purgatory. From the looks of it, there are still a few cardinals in there! Highlights include the fabulous, several-stories-tall Baroque altar El Transparente, a mixture of bronze, marble, stucco and paint. It's particularly stunning when light pours through a hole in the roof and shines on it.

You'll also find magnificent paintings, including Goya's *Arrest of Christ on the Mount of Olives* and El Greco's *Twelve Apostles*.

The Treasure Room's highlight is a 15th-century monstrance (a receptacle that holds the consecrated Host) made of gold and silver (and weighing over 400 pounds), said to have been brought by Columbus from the New World.

The sacristy holds 20 El Grecos (including his famous *The Spoliation*), Goya's *Betrayal of Christ*, and works by Velázquez, Caravaggio, Bellini, Titian, and Rubens.

Info: 1 Calle Cardenal Cisneros. Tel. 925222241. Open Mon-Sat 10am-6pm, Sun 2pm-6pm. Admission: Free to cathedral. €12.50 to visit all museums in the cathedral and the bell tower. www.catedralprimada.es.

There are several other sights worth visiting if you have the time:

The **Hospital de Tavera** was built in the 16th century for Cardinal Tavera. Now a museum housing a private art collection, it's known for its collection of paintings by El Greco, including a portrait of Cardinal Tavera. There are also paintings by Zurbarán, Tintoretto, Ribera and Titian. *Info: 2 Calle Cardinal Tavera. Tel. 925220451. Open daily 10:30am-2:30pm and 3pm-6:30pm. Admission: €6.*

When the influential Cardinal Mendoza died in the late 1400s, his riches were used to build a hospital. Its exterior is stunning, and inside the **Museo de Santa Cruz** (Santa Cruz Museum) you'll find an interesting collection of everything from archeological finds to 15th-century tapestries, antique furnishings and lots of gold. There are also paintings by Ribera, Goya and El Greco, including El Greco's incredible *Assumption of the Virgin*, painted only one year before his death in 1614. *Info: 3 Calle Miguel de Cervantes. Tel. 925221402. Open Mon-Sat 10am-6pm, 9am-3pm. Admission: €4.*

For dining, see the suggestions in *Chapter 5: Sleeping & Eating* (page 91).

EL ESCORIAL MONASTERY
San Lorenzo de El Escorial (El Escorial Monastery) is 33 miles (54 km) northwest of Madrid.

From Madrid, take the train from Atocha station. One-hour trip. From €6. 20-minute walk to town. Buses depart from Intercambiador de Moncloa (buses #664 or 661, from €4) at the metro station Moncloa. 45-minute trip. 10-minute walk to town. By car from Madrid, follow route A6 in the direction of Coruña or Villalba to exit number 47 and then San Lorenzo del Escorial exit.

El Escorial Monastery, founded by Philip II in the 16th century, is Spain's largest Renaissance structure. The granite building was constructed to provide a place where the king could live the life of a monk while ruling his empire, as he was a devout Catholic. The monastery is named after San Lorenzo (St. Lawrence), because the Spanish were victorious over the French at San Quentin on April 10, 1557, on the feast of St. Lawrence. Highlights include:

Sala de Batallas (Hall of the Battles) lined with frescoes of Spanish military victories.

Museo de Arquitectura (Museum of Architecture) telling the story of the 21 years it took to build the monastery.

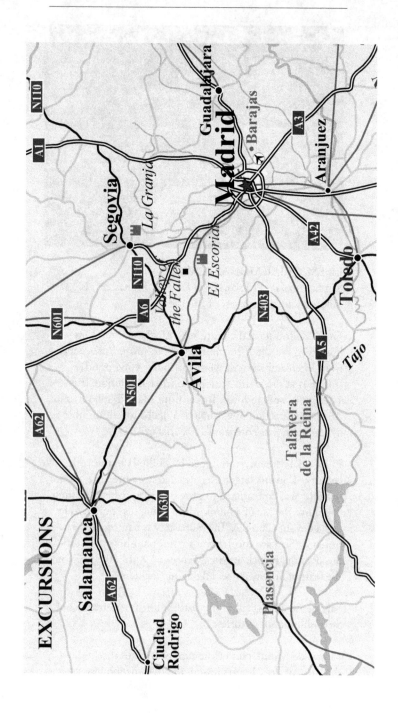

The spectacular **Basílica** has a floor plan in the shape of a Greek cross, an enormous dome, and is decorated with frescoes. The large chapel has an altarpiece with bronze sculptures. In the Capitulary and the Sacristy rooms are paintings such as *La Túnica de José* by Velázquez and *La Última Cena* (The Last Supper) by Titian. By the way, that saint engulfed in flames in the center of the altar is San Lorenzo (to whom the Basilica is dedicated), and I think you can figure out how he died at the hands of the Romans. Also in the basilica is a marble sculpture by Cellini, *The Crucifixion*.

The **Audience Chamber** is now a royal portrait gallery and believe me, those royals weren't a pretty bunch!

The **Royal Apartments** can be viewed, but quite frankly, you can breeze through these, as there isn't much of interest here.

Under the basilica is the true highlight of your visit. The **Panteón Real** (Royal Pantheon) is the burial place for the kings of Spain (and those queens who became mothers of kings). It's an octagonal Baroque mausoleum made of marble. Behind the walls of the crypt is the "rotting room" where the royal corpse remains until it rots and then it's moved to the crypt. Now there's a creepy tradition! There's a separate **Panteón de los Infantes** (Royal Children Pantheon) for children who died before receiving their first Holy Communion.

In the **Museum of Painting**, you'll find works by El Greco, Ribera, Tintoretto, Titian and Rubens.

The **Royal Library** is on the second floor and holds over 60,000 volumes, one of the most significant collections in the world. But it's not the books that most come to see, it's the vaulted ceiling decorated with frescoes by Tibaldo, inspired by Michelangelo.

Info: Tel. 918905903 (tourist-information center). Open Apr-Sep Tue-Sun 10am-8pm (Oct-Mar until 6pm). Last entry is an hour before closing. Admission: €12. www.sanlorenzodeelescorial.org.

VALLE DE LOS CAÍDOS (VALLEY OF THE FALLEN)
Valle de los Caídos (Valley of the Fallen) is 39 miles (62 km) northwest of Madrid.

Located six miles north of El Escorial. By bus from El Escorial (line 660) departing from the Plaza de la Virgen de Gracia (Autocares Herranz). By car from El Escorial take M-600. By bus from Madrid's Moncloa Intercambiador (bus 664). It's a 45-minute trip. By car from Madrid, follow route A6 in the direction of Coruña or Villalba to exit number 47 and then the Valle de los Caídos exit.

A vast basilica has been excavated inside of a mountain, on top of which looms a 500-foot-tall granite cross. The monument covers over 3,360 acres of the Sierra de Guadarrama hills.

It was built by General Francisco Franco to remember the dead of Spain's Civil War. Franco ruled Spain as a dictator for 36 years, from the end of the Spanish Civil War in 1939 until his death in 1975. He ordered construction to begin on the Valley of the Fallen only a year after the war ended, as a national act of atonement. The setting and views are quite beautiful. What isn't beautiful is that the complex was built by slave labor.

The remains of over 40,000 who died in the Civil War between 1936 and 1939 are buried here. In 1960, Pope John XXIII declared the underground crypt a basilica. The size of the basilica is larger than St. Peter's in Rome.

It served as the burial place of Franco from his death in November 1975. For years, many argued that leaving Franco's remains at The Valley of the Fallen was a celebration of his regime.

The dictator's remains were exhumed in 2019 (after years of legal and political battles) and he was laid to rest in a family cemetery north of Madrid.

There were Spaniards who came here to remember the former dictator and plenty who came to spit on his tomb. Prior to the removal of Franco's remains, the Valley of the Fallen served as a massive and somewhat creepy "monument" to fascism.

A funicular can take you to the base of the cross (round-trip €3).

Info: Tel. 918905411. Open Apr-Sep Tue-Sun 10am-7pm, Oct-Mar Tue-Sun 10am-6pm. Admission: €9.

4. WALKS

Madrid is a great place to walk. Most of the city's main sights are within easy walking distance, making Madrid a visitor-friendly place.

We'll discover some of the best sights of Madrid on two walks. Among the places you will visit are the **Palacio Real**, **Catedral de la Almudena**, and **Plaza Mayor**.

We'll also have fun discovering great places to try *tapas*. *Tapeo* is the act of bar-hopping in the early evening, eating *tapas* and drinking, before Spain's very late dinner hour. Like the Madrileños, you'll enjoy a leisurely evening and sample something you've never had before. You might discover that you actually like sardine heads.

Put on your walking shoes and get ready to experience this great city on foot!

MAJOR SIGHTS WALK I
Highlights: **Palacio Real, Catedral de la Almudena,** and **Plaza Mayor.** See map on page 72. Approximate distance one mile.

Take the metro to the Ópera stop. When you exit, you'll be in the square Plaza de Isabel II. The large building here is the back of the Royal Theater. Facing the Royal Theater, head left to the street Calle de Vergara. Turn right onto Calle de Vergara and then right onto Calle de Carlos III and head into the large square.

This square is the **Plaza de Oriente.** It's lined with statues of the kings and queens of Spain (that's Philip IV on his horse in the center of the square).

On one side of the square is the **Teatro Real** (Royal Theater). It was built in 1850 and is the site of opera and ballet performances, but the real star is the interior of the building itself. There are tours daily. www.teatro-real.com.

That huge building on the square is our next sight.

Perched on a hill overlooking the city, the **Palacio Real** (Royal Palace) has 3,000 rooms, and some are open to the public. Spaniards will proudly tell you that it's twice as large as Buckingham Palace. You can visit the rooms of King Alfonso XIII, who was the last resident until he abdicated in 1931.

72 MADRID MADE EASY

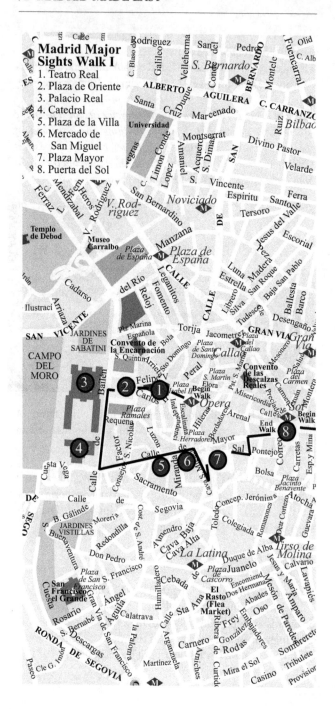

Madrid Major Sights Walk I
1. Teatro Real
2. Plaza de Oriente
3. Palacio Real
4. Catedral
5. Plaza de la Villa
6. Mercado de San Miguel
7. Plaza Mayor
8. Puerta del Sol

WALKS 73

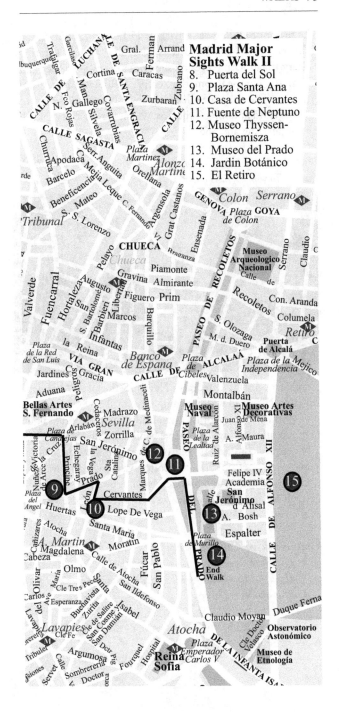

The present building dates back to 1738, and is built on the sight of a former Moorish fortress. Also, don't miss the Painting Gallery (filled with pieces by such notables as Velázquez and Goya), the Throne Room, the Reception Room and the Royal Armoury. The elaborate Changing of the Guard takes place in the courtyard at noon on the first Wednesday of every month except Jan, Aug and Sep.

With the Royal Palace to your back, head right down Calle de Bailén. To your right is our next stop, just past the Royal Palace.

Construction of the **Catedral de Nuestra Señora de la Almudena** began in 1883 and was not completed until 1993. Admission is free, so enter through the huge sculpted doors and look up at the colorful ceiling. In a chapel behind the altar is the empty 12th-century coffin of St. Isidro, the patron saint of Madrid. Forty years after he died, the coffin was opened (now, who decided to do this?) and his body had not decayed, which was enough for the pope to canonize him. He's buried elsewhere in the city.

Continue down Calle de Bailén until you reach Calle Mayor. Take a left onto Calle Mayor. Walk down the left side of the street. At Calle de la Almudena, you'll notice a bronze statue of a man looking at a glass enclosure.

The glass enclosure contains the ruins of the church **Iglesia de Nuestra Señora de la Almudena**.

Pass Calle de Factor and Calle de San Nicolás. At Calle de Calderón de la Barca, cross the street to the square.

You can experience a little bit of medieval times at the **Plaza de la Villa**. This is Madrid's oldest square, dominated by the **Casa de la Villa**, the former town hall (to your right). The building straight ahead is **Casa de Cisneros**, which dates back to 1537. To your left is the 15th-century tower **Torre de los Lujanes**.

Continue down Calle Mayor. Turn right at Plaza de San Miguel.

The iron-and-glass building here is the 1915 **Mercado de San Miguel**, filled with fresh produce, meats and lots of stinky fish.

After you've visited the market, turn right from the Plaza de San Miguel onto Cava de San Miguel.

The narrow bars that look like caves here are called *mesones*, and are an interesting place for a late-night *sangria*. This is a great area to have a drink and *tapas*.

Head down Cava de San Miguel and it turns into Calle Cuchilleros.

On the left at number 17 is **Botín**, made famous in Ernest Hemingway's *The Sun Also Rises*. You'll eat in tiled, wood-beamed dining rooms in Madrid's (and allegedly, the world's) oldest restaurant. It's quite touristy, but the food, especially roast suckling pig (*cochinillo assado*), won't disappoint. Stop here for a meal if you have the time. Moderate-Expensive.

Turn around and head back up the street to the steps leading into Madrid's grand square. On the steps up, you'll pass **Las Cuevas de Luis Candelas**, *Madrid's oldest tavern.*

The **Plaza Mayor** is an arcaded and cobblestone square dating back to 1617. It's surrounded by buildings with balconies and is truly the heart of **Viejo Madrid** (Old Madrid), and one of Europe's grandest squares. Throughout the years the square has seen everything from public executions during the Inquisition to bullfights. Notice the colorful paintings on the **Casa de la Panaderia** ("bakery") on the north side of the square. It remains a meeting place for all of Madrid, and is the sight of frequent markets and festivals. There's a huge Christmas market here in December. That's Felipe III, who ordered this square to be built, on his horse in the center of the square. Take a stroll around this grand square.

You can exit the square through the northeast corner (between numbers 31 and 32) onto the street Calle de la Sal. Turn left onto Calle de Postas. Continue on to the large square Puerta del Sol. From here you can take the Puerta del Sol metro back to your hotel, or you can continue on to our next walk.

MAJOR SIGHTS WALK II

Highlights: **Puerta del Sol**, **Museo del Prado** and **Parque del Retiro**. See map on page 73. Approximate distance one mile.

Take the metro to Puerta del Sol to begin this walk.

The **Puerta del Sol** (which means "Gateway of the Sun") is always crowded. There's a bronze plaque set into the sidewalk on the south side of the square from which all distances in Spain are measured. That statue is King Charles III (who ruled from 1759-1788) on his horse. He's facing a building that dates back to 1768 and is now the headquarters of Madrid's regional government. Check out the huge Tio Pepe sign, Madrid's first billboard. On the corner of Calle de Carmen is a bronze statue of a bear – the symbol of Madrid.

From the square, head east in the direction of the Tio Pepe sign (the street to the right of the Tio Pepe sign) on Carrera de San Jerónimo. Walk on the right side of the street.

At the corner of Calle Victoria is the **Museo del Jamón** at 6 Carrera de San Jerónimo. The "Museum of Ham" isn't really a museum, but a chain of delis serving and selling ham. You can't miss it, as you'll see hundreds of hams hanging from the ceiling. Try a glass of sherry and cured ham. There's a restaurant upstairs (where you'll pay more).

You'll pass Calle de la Cruz and then arrive at the Plaza de Canalejas. Turn right onto Calle de Principe. Head down Calle de Principe.

You'll soon run into our next sight, the **Plaza Santa Ana**. This pleasant square is located in one of Madrid's oldest neighborhoods. This is where many Madrileños congregate on weekend evenings. It's home to **Teatro Español**, the city's oldest theater dating back to 1745 (it's to your left). Across the square is the stately Hotel Reina Victoria. There are great places to take a break here, especially **Cervecería Alemana** at number 6. One street off of the square (at the end of Calle de Principe) is **Casa Alberto** at 18 Calle de las Huertas. This *taberna* and restaurant has been open since 1827. You'll have great *tapas* or main courses at reasonable prices, and the staff is exceptionally friendly. These two eateries are included in the *Tapas* Walk in this book.

Take a left onto Calle de Prado. You'll pass Calle de Echegaray and Calle de Ventura de la Vega. Turn right at Calle de León and then make a left onto Calle de Cervantes (the first street on your left).

You'll pass the **Casa de Cervantes** at the corner of Calle de Cervantes and Calle de León. This is where Cervantes, the author of *Don Quixote de la Mancha*, died. It's on the right side of the street.

Continue along Calle de Cervantes. It will turn slightly to the left at Plaza de Jesus.

You'll soon find yourself at the beautiful fountain **Fuente de Neptuno** on the Plaza de Cánovas del Castillo. The fountain is named after the Roman god of the sea. Across the square is the **Museo Thyssen-Bornemisza** at 8 Paseo del Prado. It contains an interesting and eclectic collection, acquired by the Spanish government in 1993, featuring works by Picasso, Velázquez, Goya, El Greco and Rembrandt. It also has a collection of contemporary works, including some by Pollock, Lichtenstein and Kandinsky.

Head to your right down the Paseo del Prado.

That massive museum you'll see on your left is the **Museo del Prado**, one of Europe's greatest museums, with 7,000 paintings by such notables as Velázquez, Goya, El Greco, Titian, Botticelli, Murillo and Rubens.

You can visit the museum, or if you walk past the museum, you'll see the **Jardín Botánico**, Madrid's large botanical garden (open daily at 10am). Behind the museum is **El Retiro**, a 350-acre park. It dates back to the 1630s, and is filled with statues, fountains, a lake, and lots of locals (and tourists) enjoying this vast green space in the midst of Madrid. Art is showcased in the **Palacio de Cristal** and the **Palacio de Velázquez**, 19th-century pavilions in the park. We'll end our walk here.

TAPAS WALK

Approximate distance a half-mile. See map on the next page.

The Spanish love *tapas*. They're small amounts of nearly any kind of food, usually served with a small glass of wine, beer or spirit. The time between lunch and dinner is usually when most Spaniards frequent *tapas* bars. You can have a *porción* (small sample) or a *ración* (a larger serving). Bars that serve wine, beer and snacks/appetizers (both hot and cold) are known as *tascas*. *Tapeo* is the act of bar-hopping in the early evening, eating *tapas* and drinking, before Spain's very late dinner hour.

Remember that this is meant to be a walk, not a stagger. Like the Madrileños, you should enjoy a leisurely evening. Take your time at each place. Sample something you've never had before. You might discover that you actually like sardine heads.

A few tips that will help you with this walk: Many *tapas* bars don't take credit cards, and it's usually cheaper to order at the bar rather than at a table.

Our walk begins at the **Plaza Santa Ana**. *One way to reach the square is to take the metro to the Sevilla stop on Calle de Alcalá. Head south down Calle de Sevilla to the Plaza de Canalejas. Off of this plaza, head down Calle de Principe. You'll soon run into the Plaza Santa Ana but don't stop just yet. At the square (on your left) is the Teatro Español, the city's oldest theater dating back to 1745. If you continue past the square and keep walking, you'll run into Calle de las Huertas and our first stop.*

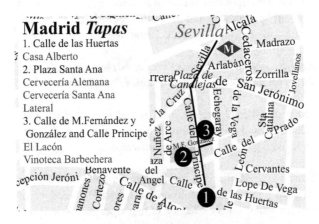

Madrid *Tapas*
1. Calle de las Huertas
   Casa Alberto
2. Plaza Santa Ana
   Cervecería Alemana
   Cervecería Santa Ana
   Lateral
3. Calle de M. Fernández y
   González and Calle Principe
   El Lacón
   Vinoteca Barbechera

At number 18 is my favorite *tapas* bar in Madrid. **Casa Alberto**, a *taberna* and restaurant, has been open since 1827. You'll have great *tapas* or main courses at reasonable prices, and the staff is exceptionally friendly. Why don't you stand at the bar and have *albóndigas de ternera* (veal meatballs). They're fabulous! Down them with a glass of *vino tinto* (red wine). *Closed Sun (dinner) and Mon. www.casaalberto.es.*

Now head back to the Plaza Santa Ana.

This pleasant square is located in one of Madrid's oldest neighborhoods. This is where many Madrileños congregate on weekend evenings. In addition to the **Teatro Español**, the square is also home to the stately Hotel Reina Victoria.

On the south side of the square are three places you can visit.

At number 6 is **Cervecería Alemana**, the best of the many *tapas* bars on the square, which was built in 1904 and modeled after a German beer hall (*Alemana* means "German" in Spanish). Have a beer. It'll be served in a white stein. Ernest Hemingway drank here, but that's really no big deal since he drank all over Madrid. Why don't you order *aceitunas* (olives), a popular snack? You'll be eating more later. *www.cerveceriaalemana.com.*
Another beer hall here is **Cervecería Santa Ana** at number 10. Here you can have a plate of *jamón y queso* (cured ham and cheese). *www.cerveceriasantaana.com.*

Another *tapas* spot here is **Lateral** at number 12. Try a glass of delicious Spanish wine and the *tortilla española* (omelette with potato and onion filling). *www.lateral.com*.

From the south side of the square, head across the square to the north side and turn right onto Calle de Manuel Fernández y González.

At number 8 is **El Lacón**. This bar and restaurant has tiled walls and wood ceiling beams. You come here to try the tasty Andalusian *gazpacho*. *www.mesonellacon.com*.

Nearby at 27 Calle Principe is **Vinoteca Barbechera**. This wine bar puts a modern spin on *tapas*. Excellent selection of Spanish wines. Try the selection of four *tapas* (*surtido 4 tapas*).

To return to where you began your walk, head back to the Plaza Santa Ana and then back up Calle de Principe to Calle Sevilla and Sevilla metro stop.

5. SLEEPING & EATING

One great way to experience life in a European city is to **rent an apartment**. They're usually less expensive and larger than a hotel room. There are many apartments for rent on the Internet. You can check out www.airbnb.com/Madrid, www.vrbo.com, and www.plumguide.com.

It cannot be stressed enough that **Spaniards eat extremely late**. The evening meal is usually served between 10pm and midnight. While some restaurants have begun to open earlier, especially in restaurants that are frequented by tourists, most Spaniards still eat late. You'll find a more genuine Spanish dining experience if you do, too.

A Word on *Tapas*

The Spanish love *tapas*. They're small amounts of nearly any kind of food, usually served with a small glass of wine, beer or spirit. The time between lunch and dinner is usually when most Spaniards frequent *tapas* bars. You can have a *porción* (small sample) or a *ración* (a larger serving). The word *tapa* means lid or cover. It's said that this tradition started in the 18th century when Carlos III asked for his wine to be covered with a plate of food to stop dust from getting into it. Bars that serve wine, beer and snacks/appetizers (both hot and cold) are known as *tascas*. *Tapeo* is the act of bar-hopping in the early evening, eating *tapas* and drinking, before Spain's very late dinner hour. Many *tapas* bars don't take credit cards, and it's usually cheaper to order at the bar rather than at a table.

SLEEPING

Ritz €€€

The Hotel Ritz in Madrid, like its sister in Paris, has a reputation as one of the grand luxury hotels in Europe. Located in a palace built in 1910, this 167-room hotel offers every amenity imaginable.

> **Sleeping Prices**
>
> Prices for two people in a double room:
> - Expensive: over €200
> - Moderate: €100-200
> - Inexpensive: under €100

It's located within blocks of two of Madrid's famous museums: The Prado and Thyssen-Bornemisza. Even if you don't stay here, you can drop quite a few euros at its five restaurants and bars. *Info: 4 Plaza de la Lealtad. Tel. 917016767. www.mandarinoriental.com/madrid. V, MC, AE. Restaurants, bar, gym, room service, Satellite TV, AC, telephone, minibar, hairdryer, in-room safe. Metro: Banco de España.*

Reina Victoria €€€

The stately Reina Victoria sits on one of the most fun squares in Madrid, the Plaza Santa Ana (a popular place to sample *tapas*). The hotel reopened in October of 2006 after an extensive renovation, including soundproofed windows (a necessity because of the hotel's location on the noisy square. Excellent location and friendly staff. *Info: 14 Plaza Santa Ana. Tel. 917016000. www.melia.com. V, MC, AE. Restaurant, bar, room service, gym, satellite TV, AC, telephone, minibar, hairdryer, in-room safe, Wi-Fi Internet access. Metro: Sevilla or Sol.*

Hotel Villa Real €€-€€€

This luxury hotel, popular with business travelers, is located in a renovated 19th-century building adjacent to the Spanish Parliament and only three blocks from the Prado. Rave reviews for service. Rooms are large and comfortable with marble bathrooms and furniture crafted from mahogany or olive-tree root. It's website offers frequent deals. *Info: 10 Plaza de las Cortes. Tel. 914203767. www.hotelvillareal.com. V, MC, AE. Two restaurants, bar, gym, room service, Satellite TV, AC, telephone, minibar, hairdryer, in-room safe. Metro: Sevilla or Banco de España.*

Quatro €€

This sleek and modern 62-room hotel has an excellent location near the Puerta del Sol. Friendly service. *Info: 4 Calle Sevilla. Tel. 915329049. www.hotelquatropuertadelsol.com. V, MC, AE. Restaurant, bar, room service, satellite TV, AC, telephone, minibar, hairdryer, in-room safe, Wi-Fi Internet access. Metro: Sevilla or Sol.*

SLEEPING & EATING 85

Hotel Meninas €€
This 37-room hotel is named after the painting by Velázquez that hangs in the Prado Museum, is located in a refurbished 19th-century townhouse near the Teatro Real, so it's in the middle of everything. Soundproof windows help keep the bustle out. *Info: 7 Calle Campomanes. Tel. 915412805. Metro Ópera. www.hotelmeninasmadrid.es. V, MC, AE. Bar, flat-screen satellite TV, AC, telephone, in-room safe, minibar, hairdryer, dvd player, WiFi.*

Suite Prado €€
This apartment/hotel has a good location near the *tapas* bars on Plaza Santa Ana and not too far from the Prado Museum. Studio apartments and suites all have marble bathrooms and small kitchenettes. Especially good for families. *Info: 10 Calle de Manuel Fernández y González. Tel. 914202318. www.suiteprado.com. V, MC, AE. Cable TV, AC, telephone, Wi-Fi access. Metro: Sevilla.*

IBIS Styles Madrid Prado Hotel €€
This 47-room hotel has clean, modern rooms and a great location near the Museo Thyssen-Bornemisza and the *tapas* bars of the Plaza Santa Ana. *Info: 11 Calle Prado. Tel. 913690234. www.allaccor.com. V, MC. Satellite TV, AC, telephone, minibar, limited room service, bar, parking available. Metro: Banco de España.*

Hostal Madrid Sol €
Streamlined rooms with contemporary decor. Bathrooms have shower stalls. Good location near the *tapas* bars on Plaza Santa Ana and the major sights. Museo del Prado, Reina Sofia, Thyssen-Bornemisza, Plaza de Cibeles, Almudena Cathedral, and the Royal Palace are all within walking distance. *Info: 18 Calle del Príncipe. Tel. 915313270. www.hostal-madridsol.com. V, MC. AC, WiFi. Metro: Sol.*

Hotel Mora €
A favorite of travelers for years, you can't beat its location across the street from the Prado Museum. Its 60 rooms are mid-sized and comfortable and have soundproof windows. If you're traveling by train, the Atocha station (with its beautiful tropical garden inside) is located nearby. *Info: 32 Paseo del Prado. Tel. 914201569. www.hotelmora.com. V, MC, AE. AC, TV, telephone, in-room safe. Metro: Atocha.*

Hostal Triana €
This basic hostel located near the Gran Vía and Sol metro stops has 40 basic rooms. You can reach most major attractions on foot. No breakfast service, but there are plenty of cafés nearby. Air-conditioning is available in some rooms at an additional cost. *Info: 13 Calle Salud. Tel. 915326812. www.hostaltriana.com. V, MC. TV, telephone, WiFi. Metro: Gran Vía or Sol.*

TOLEDO

Parador de Toledo €€
Unlike most *paradores* in Spain, this one (on the outskirts of town) is modern. Excellent restaurant and wonderful views of Toledo. Best for those traveling by car. You'll need reservations well in advance. Fabulous bathrooms. *Info: Cerro del Emperador. Tel. 925221850. www.parador.es. V, MC, AE. Restaurant, bar, pool, TV, AC, hair dryer, in-room safe, free parking, WiFi.*

Hotel Alfonso VI €-€€
A favorite of mine. I first stayed at this 83-room hotel in the 1990s. The location, in the middle of Old Town, is perfect for exploring the city. Great views from the terrace. Good restaurant. *Info: 2 General Moscardó. Tel. 925222600. www.hotelalfonsovi.com. V, MC, AE. Restaurant, bar, TV, AC, hair dryer, in-room safe, WiFi.*

Hacienda del Cardenal €-€€
A friendly staff, one of the best restaurants in town and lovely gardens all make this hotel an excellent choice. It's located in the former 18th-century summer palace of Cardinal Lorenzana. The entry is through the ancient city walls. *Info: 24 Paseo Recaredo. Tel. 925224900. www.haciendadelcardenal.com. V, MC, AE. Restaurant, bar, TV, AC, hair dryer, in-room safe, WiFi.*

Hotel Imperio €
The budget choice in Toledo. The small rooms all have private baths. The location, near the cathedral and Alcázar, is perfect for sightseeing. Some of the balconies offer great views of the Alcázar and Toledo. *Info: 5 Calle Horno de Los Bizcochos. Tel. 925280034. www.hoteltoledoimperial.com. V, MC, AE. TV, AC, WiFi.*

EATING

Phone numbers, days closed and hours of operation often change, so it's advisable to check ahead. Restaurants in tourist areas may have different hours and days of operation during low season. Reservations are recommended for all restaurants unless noted. The telephone country code for Spain is 34.

Prices are for main courses. Lunch, even at the most expensive restaurants listed below, always has a lower fixed price. Credit cards are accepted unless noted otherwise. We have listed the nearest metro stop.

Dining Prices

Prices for a main course:
- €€€€ Very Expensive: over €30
- €€€ Expensive: €21-€30
- €€ Moderate: €10-€20
- € Inexpensive: under €10

MADRID

Bocaíto €€
Tapas and Spanish specialties at this tiled bar/restaurant. *Tapas* cost between €2 and €8 and there's a tasting menu for €35. Prices are cheaper if you sit at the bar. *Info: 6 Calle de Libertad. Tel. 915321219. Closed Sun and most of Aug. Metro: Banco de España or Chueca. www.bocaito.com.*

Botín €€-€€€
Made famous in Ernest Hemingway's *The Sun Also Rises*. You'll eat in tiled, wood-beamed dining rooms in Madrid's (and allegedly, the world's) oldest restaurant. It's quite touristy, but the food, especially roast suckling pig (*cochinillo assado*), won't disappoint. *Info: 17 Calle Cuchilleros. Tel. 913664217. Open daily. Metro: Puerta del Sol or La Latina. www.botin.es.*

Cebo €€€
This modern and award-winning restaurant is located in the Hotel Urban not too far from the Museo Thyssen-Bornemisza. There are two menu options. The classic menu has ten courses (€80). The interesting *Menú Las Diecisiete* (Menu The Seventeen) offers 17 courses, one for each of the 17 regions of Spain (€110). A modern spin on Spanish cuisine. *Info: 34 Carrera de San Jerónimo. Tel. 917877780. Closed Sun, Mon and most of Aug. Metro: Sevilla. www.cebomadrid.com.*

Casa Lucio €€-€€€
Spanish cuisine in an attractive setting (tiled floors, exposed brick walls and hams hanging from the ceiling). A specialty at this popular restaurant is *churrasco* (thick grilled steak). If it's good enough for former King Juan Carlos and Bill Clinton, it should be good enough for you. *Info: 35 Cava Baja. Tel. 913653252. Closed Aug. Metro: La Latina. www.casalucio.es.*

Casa Paco €€-€€€
After a shot of red wine at the zinc-topped bar, you order steaks by weight in the tiled dining rooms. Grilled lamb and fish are also served. *Info: 11 Plaza de Puerta Cerrada. Tel. 913663167. Closed Sun and Aug. Reservations required. Metro: La Latina. www.casapaco1933.es.*

Las Cuevas de Luis Candelas €€-€€€
Okay, so it's touristy with its strolling musicians and host dressed like a bandit. But this "cave" off of the Plaza Mayor is the oldest tavern in Madrid. *Tapas* and dining (especially barbecued meats). *Info: 1 Calle Cuchilleros. Tel. 913665428. Open daily. Metro: Puerta del Sol or La Latina. www.lascuevasdeluiscandelas.es.*

La Gamella €€-€€€
A little bit of the U.S. at this popular restaurant with good service and innovative cuisine. Delicious hamburgers and there's a popular Sunday brunch. Try the *medallones de solomillo* (tenderloin medallions). *Info: 4 Calle de Alfonso XII. Tel. 915324509. No dinner Sun. Metro: Retiro. www.lagamella.com.*

El Mirador del Museo €€-€€€
International and Spanish dishes are served under the stars on the top floor of the Museo Thyssen-Bornemisza. A truly unique experience. Good wine list. *Info: 8 Paseo del Prado. Tel 914293984. Open Jul and Aug. Closed Sun. Reservations required. Metro: Banco de España. www.elmiradordethyssen.com.*

Spanish Menu Help

You'll eat *pintxos* and *criadillas*... and like them!
Reading a menu in Spanish can be confusing.
For a comprehensive **Spanish menu translator**, get our
Eating & Drinking in Spain and Portugal book!

Los Montes de Galicia €€-€€€
This attractive restaurant and bar is located in the Salamanca neighborhood and serves the specialties of the region of Galicia. The menu emphasizes seafood, so try the *buñuelos de bacalao* (fried pastry with dried salted cod) or the *pulpo a fiera* (octopus with paprika). If you're not in the mood for seafood, try the tasty *vaca gallega* (sirloin from Galicia). *Info: 46 Calle Azcona. Tel. 913552786. Open daily. Metro: Ventas or Diego de Léon. www.losmontesdegalicia.es.*

Vinos de Bellota €€
This casual, friendly, and often crowded wine bar/restaurant is located near the Parque del Retiro. Start with the *croquetas* (croquettes) or the interesting *crema de morcilla* (black pudding cream). Delicious baked *merluza* (hake) dish. Good selection of Spanish wines (especially Rioja). *Info: 27 Antonio Acuna/3 Doctor Castelo. Tel. 912092636. Closed Mon. Metro: Ibiza or Ppe. de Vergara. www.vinosdebellota.com.*

La Taberna del Alabardero €-€€€
Near the Royal Palace and El Teatro Real, this small and charming *taberna* serves *tapas*, and has a wonderful restaurant in the back room serving Spanish and Basque cuisine. The pheasant (*faisán*) is great. *Info: 6 Calle de Felipe V. Tel. 915472577. Open daily. Metro: Ópera. Tapas(€). Restaurant (€€€). www.alabarderomadrid.es.*

Casa Mingo €-€€
You'll share sausages, roast chicken and salad at long tables with other diners at this *bodega* (tavern). Cider (*sidra*) is the drink of choice here. Not to be missed! *Info: 34 Paseo de la Florida (across the street from Goya's tomb). Tel. 915477918. Open daily 11am-midnight. No reservations. No credit cards. Metro: Príncipe Pío (about a 10-minute walk from the metro stop). www.casamingo.es.*

MADRID MARKETS/FOOD AND WINE STORES
Mercado de San Miguel
This iron-and-glass building, built in 1915, is filled with fresh produce, meats, stinky fish, and lots of *tapas* stands. *Info: Plaza de San Miguel (off of Calle Mayor) near Plaza Mayor. Tel. 915424936. Open daily 10am to midnight (Fri and Sat until 1am). Metro: Ópera. www.mercadodesanmiguel.es.*

Chocolatería San Ginés
This 100-year-old *chocolateria* is where you can sample chocolate *churros y porras*. *Churros* are loops and *porras* are sticks of deep-fried batter which you dip in hot chocolate. *Info: 5 Pasadizo de San Ginés (an alleyway off of Calle del Arenal). Tel. 913656546. Open daily 24 hours. Metro: Ópera or Puerta del Sol. www.chocolateriasangines.com.*

Mallorca
Open since the 1930s, this food and wine shop sells Spanish food specialties and a selection of Spanish wines. You can inexpensively sample the food at the *tapas* bar. There are several locations throughout the city. *Info: 6 Calle de Serrano (at Calle de Columela). Tel. 915771859. Open daily 9am-9pm. Metro: Retiro. www.pasteleria-mallorca.com.*

MADRID *TAPAS* BARS
Head to the Plaza Santa Ana. All of these *tapas* bars are within walking distance of each other. Many are closed in August.

Casa Alberto
Our favorite place for *tapas* in Madrid. This *taberna* and restaurant has been open since 1827. You'll have great *tapas* or main courses at reasonable prices, and the staff is exceptionally friendly. Why don't you stand at the bar and have *albóndigas de ternera* (veal meatballs)? They're fabulous! Down them with a glass of *vino tinto* (red wine). *Info: 18 Calle de las Huertas. Tel. 914299356. Closed Mon. and after 4pm Sun. www.casaalberto.es.*

Cervecería Alemana
The best of the many *tapas* bars on the square, built in 1904 and modeled after a German beer hall (*Alemana* means "German" in Spanish). Have a beer. It'll be served in a white stein. Ernest Hemingway drank here, but that's really no big deal since he drank all over Madrid. Why don't you order *aceitunas* (olives), a popular snack? You'll be eating more later. *Info: 6 Plaza de Santa Ana. Tel. 914297033. Closed Tue. www.cerveceriaalemana.com.*

Lateral
Try a glass of delicious Spanish wine and the *tortilla española* (omelette with potato and onion filling). *Info: 12 Plaza de Santa Ana. Tel. 914201582. Open daily. www.lateral.com.*

Viva Madrid
You come here to drink, and it's likely that the crowd will be lively. Fantastic tiled walls and an incredible carved ceiling. Try the delicious *chuletas de cordero* (lamb chops). *Info: 7 Calle de Manuel Fernández y González. Tel. 916059774. Closed Mon.*

Museo del Jamón
The "Museum of Ham" isn't really a museum, but a chain of delis serving and selling ham. It's not hard to notice the delis as you'll see hundreds of hams hanging from the ceiling. Try a glass of sherry and cured

ham. *Info: 72 Calle Gran Vía. Tel. 915412023. Open daily. Metro: Plaza de España. Also at 54 Calle Atocha. Tel. 913692204. Open daily. Metro: Antón Martín. www.museodeljamon.es.*

TOLEDO
Restaurante la Orza €€€
This cozy restaurant with stone walls is located in the Jewish Ghetto near the Casa del Greco. Start with the interesting *crêpes de morcilla* (black-pudding crêpes). For dinner, try the *bacalao pil-pil* (cod casserole with garlic and olive oil) or the *venado* (venison). End you meal with the tasty *mazapán* (marzipan) dessert. *Info: 5 Calle Descalzos. Tel. 925223011. Closed Sun (dinner). www.restaurantelaorza.com*

L'Ermita €€€
You don't just come here to dine. The view of the city (especially when lit at night) is spectacular. The restaurant is located on a cliff across the river from the city. Try the delicious *solomillo de ternera* (veal tenderloin) or the *rodaballo* (turbot). Excellent selection of local wines. *Info: Ermita de Nuestra Senora del Valle - Ctra Circunvalación. Tel. 925253193. Closed Sun. (dinner) and Mon. www.lermitarestaurante.com.*

Alfileritos 24 €-€€€
This appealing bar (€) and restaurant (€€€) serves *tapas* and local specialties. The *taberna* (bar) is downstairs and the restaurant is upstairs. Try the *ciervo* (venison). Ample selection of Spanish wines by the glass and bottle. Helpful staff. *Info: 24 Alfileritos (at Calle Cristo de la Luz). Tel. 925239625. www.alfileritos24.com.*

Eating & Drinking

LET'S DRINK	TOP *TAPAS*
wine, *vino*	*tortilla española*, omelette with potato and onion
beer, *cerveza*	*jamón serrano*, cured ham
glass, *vaso*	*albóndigas*, meatballs
bottle, *botella*	*almendras*, almonds
cheers, *salud*	*mejillones*, mussels
wine list, *carta de vinos*	*gambas*, shrimp
wine (red), *vino tinto*	*chorizo*, cured sausage
wine (rosé), *vino rosado/rosé*	*olivas*, olives
wine (white), *vino blanco*	

Tips For Budget Dining

There is no need to spend a lot of money in Madrid to have good food. There are all kinds of fabulous foods to be had inexpensively all over the city.

Eat at a neighborhood restaurant or *tapas* bar. You'll usually know the price of a meal before entering, as almost all restaurants post the menu and prices in the window. Never order anything whose price is not known in advance unless you're feeling adventurous.

Delis and food stores can provide cheap and wonderful meals. Buy some cheese, bread, wine and other snacks and have a picnic. Remember to pack a corkscrew and eating utensils when you leave home.

The Spanish eat very late. Sometimes when you go to a *tapas* bar (or several) before dinner, you find that you really aren't up to a late-night dinner.

Lunch, even at the most expensive restaurants listed in this guide, always has a lower price. So, have lunch as your main meal.

Restaurants that have menus written in English (especially those near tourist attractions) are almost always more expensive than neighborhood restaurants.

If you're concerned about the cost of a meal, the menu of the day *menú del dia* is usually a better value for your money than purchasing food á la carte.

Street vendors generally sell inexpensive and good food. For the cost of a cup of coffee or a drink, you can linger at a café and watch the world pass you by for as long as you want. It's one of Europe's greatest bargains.

And don't eat at McDonald's, for God's sake.

6. ACTIVITIES

MADRID SHOPPING
Antiques
If you're looking for antiques you'll find many dealers on Calle Ribera de Curtidores (the main street of the El Rasto flea market). There are also plenty of other antique shops on nearby streets such as Calle de Carnero and Calle Mira el Río Alta.

Department Store
El Corte Inglés
This is *the* department store in Madrid and all of Spain. In addition to clothing and household goods, check out the supermarket on the lower level. There are branches throughout the city. *Info: 1-4 Calle de Preciados. Tel. 913798000. Open Mon-Sat 10am-10pm, Sun 11am-9pm. Metro: Puerta del Sol. www.elcorteingles.es.*

Fashion
Delitto e Castigo
Luxury fashion store for men and women with names such as Balmain, Cavalli, Watanabe, Marchesa, and Ferretti. *Info: 26 Claudio Coello. Tel. 915777729. www.delittoecastigo.com.*

Food and Wine
Mallorca
Open since the 1930s, this food and wine shop sells Spanish food specialties and a selection of Spanish wines. You can inexpensively sample the food at the tapas bar. There are several locations throughout the city, including 12 Calle de Génova and 59 Calle de Velázquez. *Info: 6 Calle de Serrano (at Calle de Columela). Tel. 915771859. Open daily. Metro: Retiro.*

Market
El Rasto
For over 500 years, madrileños have headed to this massive market (near San Isidro) on Sunday mornings. It's filled with everything from used clothing to jewelry. A great place to find a cheap souvenir. Don't come here if you don't like crowds, as the market is absolutely packed with people.

And watch your wallet! *Info: Calle Ribera de Curtidores (between Ronda de Toledo and Plaza de Cascorro). Open Sunday from about 9am-2pm. Admission: Free. Metro: La Latina.*

Market (Food)
Mercado de San Miguel
The iron-and-glass building is the 1915 Mercado de San Miguel, filled with fresh produce, meats and lots of stinky fish. *Info: Plaza de San Miguel (off of Calle Mayor) near Plaza Mayor. Metro: Ópera or Sol.*

Spanish Goods
Casa Hernanz
Handmade *espadrilles* (two pieces of sturdy cotton hand-sewn to a flat hemp sole) of every size and color. What a great souvenir. The attractive *espadrille* shop (*alpargatería*) has a sales counter that dates back to the 19th century. *Info: 18 Calle de Toledo. Tel. 913665450. Closed Sun. Metro: La Latina or Tirso de Molina.*

Capas Seseña
The place in Madrid to purchase a Spanish cape. They're cut and sown by hand at this family-owned shop. Now where are you going to wear a cape back home? Oh, get ready to pay up to 1,000 euros. *Info: 23 Calle de la Cruz. Tel. 915316840. Closed Sun. www.sesena.com.*

Porcelain
Lladró
The prestigious handcrafted porcelain maker has a shop in Madrid. *Info: 76 Serrano, Tel. 914355112. Closed Sun. www.lladro.com.*

MADRID NIGHTLIFE AND ENTERTAINMENT

Bullfights
Plaza de Toros de las Ventas
It's certainly not for everyone, but attending a bullfight (*corrida*) is the quintessential Spanish experience. The free Museo Taurino (Bullfighting Museum) is also here. *Info: 237 Calle de Alcalá. Tel. 917263570. Open: Sun Mar-Oct. Box office open Fri-Sun 10am-2pm and 5pm-8pm. Admission: Begins at €11. Metro: Ventas.*

Dance Club
Kapital
Seven levels, each with its own music, in a former theater. *Info: 125 Calle Atocha. Tel. 914202906. www.teatrokapital.com. Open Thu-Sun midnight-6am. Expensive drinks!*

Flamenco
Corral de la Morería
This touristy nightclub with Arab décor has nightly *flamenco* dancing performances. As you would expect in this late-night city, many shows don't begin until late in the evening. *Info: 17 Calle de la Morería. Tel. 913658446. Open daily. Shows begin at 7:30pm. Admission: €50 (includes one drink). Dinner also available. www.corraldelamoreria.com. Metro: La Latina.*

Casa Patas
Authentic *flamenco* performances without all the glitz and tourists. *Info: 10 Calle de Cañizares. Tel. 913690496. Shows Mon-Thu at 10:30pm, Fri-Sat 8pm and 10:30pm. Admission: €40 (includes one drink). www.casapatas.com. Metro: Antón Martín.*

Gay Establishments/LGBTQ
Spain has become a leader in gay rights, including the right to marry, and Madrid is a very gay-friendly destination. Many gay establishments are found in the Chueca neighborhood (Metro: Chueca). Some gay establishments are:

The Paso, 1 Costanilla de los Capuchinos (bar-men)
Truco, 10 Calle de Gravína (bar-women)
You & Me, 6 Calle de San Bartolomé (dance club)
Zarpa, 26 Calle de las Infantas (bear bar)
boyberry Madrid, 3 Calle Vaverde (cruise club-men)
Naked Bar, 5 Calle Monteleón (naked club-men)
Sauna Beach, 9 Plaza de los Mostenses (Thu-Mon/sauna-men)
Mama Inés, 2 Calle de Hortaleza (restaurant)

Vermut
Need a break? It's a tradition in Madrid, especially on Sunday afternoons, to have a glass of vermouth (vermut) (white wine blended with herbs and fruit peels and fortified with brandy). You can take part in this tradition at the bars at the Plaza de Puerta Cerrada, just south of the Plaza Mayor.

MADRID SPORTS & RECREATION
Golf
La Herrería Club is an 18-hole course near the Monastery of San Lorenzo del Escorial. *Info: Ctra. Robledo de Chavela in Escorial. Tel. 918905111. www.golflaherreria.com. Green fees from €100.*

Running
Runners and joggers should head to Parque del Oeste or El Retiro.

Soccer
Madrid has several professional teams, including Real Madrid that plays at the massive Estadio Santiago Bernabéu. *Info: 140 Paseo de la Castellana. Tel. 913984300. www.realmadrid.es.*

Swimming
You can still swim in landlocked Madrid. The city has many indoor and outdoor swimming pools that are open to visitors. Try Piscina Canal Isabel II. Info: Ave. de Filipinas (at Plaza Juan Zorrilla). Tel. 915331791. Admission: €6. Metro: Canal or Ríos Rosas.

7. PLANNING YOUR TRIP

GETTING AROUND MADRID

Arrivals
Flights arrive at Barajas International Airport. There's a tourist information center at the airport. The metro connects with the airport in Terminals 2 and 4 from 6am-2am. It's a long (indoor) walk from the terminal to the metro stop. It's a 12-minute ride to the Nuevos Ministerios metro stop in central Madrid. Cost to central Madrid is €5. Madrid's **metro** system is the easiest way to get around. Prices are €1.50 for a single trip or €12.20 for 10 trips. They're also valid on the bus system (except the bus to and from the airport). **Exprés Aeropuerto buses** run between the airport and central Madrid about every 10-15 minutes. The bus stops at O'Donell, Plaza de Cibeles and Atocha stations. 24-hour service. Atocha stop is only between 6am and 11:30pm. The trip costs €5 and takes between 45 minutes to an hour. A taxi from the airport to central Madrid costs €30 (fixed rate). Madrid's two **train** stations, Chamartín and Atocha, are both on metro lines with access to the city center. Both train stations have tourist information centers.

Car Rental
If you're only visiting Madrid, you really don't need a car. There's good public transportation (see above). If you're planning to visit other areas, it's easiest to rent a car. Although there's extensive train and bus service, renting a car allows you the flexibility of visiting Spain's smaller towns.

Taxis
Taxis are plentiful in Spain's larger cities. Only use taxis that display a special license. Most display a green light when free (*libre*). You can flag a taxi down in the street or look for a taxi stand. Taxis are metered and may have set prices for certain journeys. Tipping is uncommon and rarely more than 5%.

Trains
High-speed trains, Alta Velocidad Español or AVE, run between major tourist destinations (Barcelona, Madrid, Seville, Toledo). Timetables, prices, and locations of stations can be found on Spain's RENFE train site www.renfe.es (in English). You can buy tickets online.

An easy way to get between Barcelona and Madrid is to take the high-speed AVE train. The trip takes about three hours and travels from Barcelona's Sants Station. Tickets cost from from €60, but pricing varies by season. Tickets can be purchased through www.raileurope.com. Budget train AVLO has frequent deals and smaller seats. www.avlorenfe.com.

PRACTICAL MATTERS

Banking & Changing Money
The euro (€) is the currency of Spain and most of Europe. Before you leave for Spain, it's a good idea to get some euros. It makes your arrival a lot easier. Call your credit-card company or bank before you leave to tell them that you'll be using your ATM or credit card outside the country. Many have automatic controls that can "freeze" your account if the computer program determines that there are charges outside your normal area. ATMs (with fees, of course) are the easiest way to change money in Spain. You'll find them everywhere, including the airports. Most ATMs have instructions in English. Beware that many establishments no longer accept traveler's checks because of fear of counterfeit checks.

Hotel and restaurant prices are required by law to include taxes and service charges. Value Added Tax (VAT) is included in the price of goods. Foreigners are entitled to a refund, but must fill out a refund form. When you make your purchase, you should ask for the form and instructions. There's a refund office at the airport. Yes, it can be a hassle. Check www.globalrefund.com for the latest information on refunds and help for a fee.

Business Hours
Business hours are generally 9:00am to 6:00pm Monday through Friday. Banks are open Monday through Friday, and some are open on Saturday mornings. Department stores are generally open 10:00am to 8:00pm Monday through Saturday. Many smaller businesses and shops close for several hours in the afternoon from 2:00pm to 4:00pm or 5:00pm.

Climate & Weather
Average high temperature/low temperature/days of rain:

Madrid:
January: 47º/35º/8
February: 52º/36º/7
March: 59º/41º/10

April: 65º/45º/9
May: 70º/50º/10
June: 80º/58º/5
July: 87º/63º/2
August: 85º/63º/3
September: 77º/57º/6
October: 65º/49º/8
November: 55º/42º/9
December: 48/36º/10
You should check www.weather.com before you leave.

Consulates & Embassies
- U.S. Embassy in Madrid: 75 Calle Serrano, Tel. 915872200
- Canadian Embassy in Madrid: 259D Paseo de Castellana, Tel. 913828400
- UK Consultate in Madrid: 259D Paseo de Castellana, Tel. 917146300

Electricity
The electrical current in Spain is 220 volts as opposed to 110 volts found at home. Don't fry your electric razor, hairdryer or laptop. You'll need a converter and an adapter. Some laptops don't require a converter, but why are you bringing one anyway? You're on vacation, remember?

Emergencies & Safety
Don't wear a "fanny pack;" it's a sign that you're a tourist and an easy target (especially in crowded tourist areas). Avoid wearing expensive jewelry. Be aware of your surroundings, especially when in large crowds.

Check with your health-care provider. Most policies don't cover you overseas. If that's the case, you may want to obtain medical insurance. Given the uncertainties in today's world, you may also want to purchase trip-cancellation insurance (for insurance coverage, check out www.insuremytrip.com). Make sure that your policy covers sickness, disasters, bankruptcy and State Department travel restrictions and warnings. In other words, read the fine print!

Festivals & Holidays in Spain
- New Year's: January 1
- Epiphany: January 6
- Andalucía Day (Andalusia): February 28
- Good Friday (movable date)
- Easter (movable date)
- Easter Monday (movable date)
- Labor Day: May 1

- Madrid Day (Madrid): May 2
- San Isidro (Madrid): May 15
- Pentecost (movable date)
- St. John's (Barcelona): June 24
- Assumption of the Virgin Mary: August 15
- Catalonia National Holiday (Barcelona): September 11
- La Mercè (Barcelona): September 23/24
- National Day: October 12
- All Saints': November 1
- Spanish Constitution Day: December 6
- Immaculate Conception: December 8
- Christmas: December 25
- Christmas Monday (Barcelona): December 26

Internet Access/WiFi
Internet cafés seem to pop up everywhere (and go out of business quickly). You shouldn't have difficulty finding a place to e-mail home. The going rate is about €3 per hour. WiFi is available at many hotels, bars, cafes, and restaurants.

Language
Although many younger Spaniards speak English, this book has a list of helpful Spanish phrases. It's always courteous to learn at least a few of them.

Packing
Never pack prescription drugs, eyeglasses or valuables. Carry them on. Think black. It always works for men and women. Oh, and by the way, pack light. Don't ruin your trip by having to lug around huge suitcases. Before you leave home, make copies of your passport, airline tickets and confirmation of hotel reservations. You should also make a list of your credit-card numbers and the telephone numbers for your credit-card companies. If you lose any of them (or they're stolen), you can call someone at home and have them provide the information to you. You should also pack copies of these documents separate from the originals.

Passport Regulations
Citizens of the United States who have been away more than 48 hours can bring home $800 of merchandise duty-free every 30 days. For more information, go to Traveler Information ("Know Before You Go") at www.cbp.gov. Canadians can bring back C$800 each year if gone for 48 hours or more. You'll need a valid passport to enter Spain from the United States and Canada for visits under three months. No visa is required.

Postal Services
Look for the "Los Correos" signs, the name for the Spanish postal system. Expect to wait in line. Stores with a brown-and-yellow "tabaco" signs sell stamps for the same price as the post office.

Restrooms
There aren't a lot of public restrooms. If you need to go, your best bet is to head (no pun intended) to the nearest café. It's considered good manners to purchase something if you use the restroom. If there's an attendant, tip up to €0.50.

Smoking
Does everyone in Spain smoke? Sometimes it seems so. Smoking is prohibited in hotels, restaurants, bars, clubs, museums and on public transportation. Smoking outdoors is also restricted in certain areas.

Telephones
- Country code for Spain: 34
- Calling Spain from the United States and Canada: Dial 011-34 plus the number in this book (which includes both the area code and local number)
- Calling the United States or Canada from Spain: Dial 00 (wait for the tone), dial 1 plus the area code and seven-digit local number
- Calling within Spain: Dial the number in this book

Phone cards purchased in Spain are the cheapest way to call. A good way to stay in touch and save money is to rent an international cell phone. One provider is www.cellhire.com. If you're a frequent visitor to Europe, you may want to purchase a cell phone (for about $50) from www.mobal.com. You'll get an international telephone number and pay by the minute for calls made on your cell phone.

If you are using your smartphone in Spain, make sure to turn off your international roaming (and use WiFi instead) to save money.

Time
When it's noon in New York City, it's 6 p.m. in Spain. For hours of events or schedules, Spaniards use the 24-hour clock. So 6am is 0600, and 1pm is 1300.

Tipping

Restaurants automatically include a tax and service charge. Depending on the service, it's *sometimes* appropriate to leave up to 5%. Travelers from the U.S. have trouble not tipping. Remember, you do *not* have to tip. It's still customary to leave a small tip unless the service or the food has been unsatisfactory. Most locals round up to the next euro and it's okay if that is what you do, too. If you want to be safe, ask if the tip is included. (*¿Esta incluida la propina?*). You may want to leave the tip in cash. A tip added to your credit-card bill does not always end up in the pocket of the server.

It's common to round up with taxi drivers. So, if the bill is €7.50, give the driver €8. If a doorman calls a cab for you, tip €1 to €1.50. Tip coat check €0.50 to €1. Bellhops expect €1 per bag.

Tourist Information
There are many helpful Tourist information Centers in Madrid, including:
- Terminals 2 and 4 at the airport
- Plaza Mayor
- Royal Palace
- Paseo de Prado
- Reina Sofia Museum

Water
Tap water is safe in Spain.

Web Sites
- Europe Made Easy Travel Guides: www.eatndrink.com
- Madrid: es.madrid.com
- Spain: www.spain.info
- U.S. State Department: www.state.gov

Siesta!

The **siesta** is alive and well in Spain. Many shops and museums close for two hours or more at lunch time, especially in the south. Plan accordingly!

ESSENTIAL PHRASES

please, por favor (*por fah-bor*)
thank you, gracias (*grah-thee-ahs*)
you are welcome, de nada (*deh-nah-da*)
yes, sí (*see*)
no, no (*no*)
good day, buenos días (*bway-nohs dee-ahs*)
good afternoon/evening, buenas tardes (*bway-nahs tar-days*)
good night, buenas noches (*bway-nahs noh-chays*)
hello, hola (*oh-la*)
goodbye, adiós (*ah-dee-ohs*)
I am sorry, lo siento (*low see-en-toh*)

do you speak English?, ¿habla usted inglés? (*ah-blah oo-stehd een-glays*)
excuse me, perdóneme (*pehr-doh-nay-may*)
I don't understand, no comprendo (*no kohm-prehn-doh*)
help, ayuda (*a-yoo-dah*)

where is...?, ¿donde esta...? (*dohn-day ay-stah*)
the train station, estación de trenes (*lah ay-stah-thee-ohn day tray-nays*)
the bus station, estación de autobuses (*lah ay-stah-thee-ohn day ow-toh-boo-says*)
where are...?, ¿donde están...? (*dohn-day ay-stahn*)
the toilets, los servicios (*lohs sehr-bee-thee-ohs*)

men, hombres (*ohm-brays*)
women, mujeres (*moo-heh-rays*)
Mr., señor (*sayn-yor*)
Mrs., señora (*sayn-yoh-rah*)
Miss, señorita (*sayn-yoh-ree-tah*)

waiter, camarero (*kah-mah-ray-roh*)
waitress, camarera (*kah-mah-ray-rah*)

what, qué (*kay*)
when, cuándo (***kwahn***-*do*)
how, como (***koh***-*mo*)
who, quién (*kee-****ehn***)
why, por qué (*por kay*)
this, esto (***ay***-*stoh*)

I'd like…, quiero… (*kee-****ehr***-*oh*)
the bill, la cuenta (*la ****kwayn***-*tah*)
a room, una habitación (*oo-nah ah-bee-tah-thee-****ohn***)
a ticket, el billete (*bee yay-tay*)
a table, una mesa (*oo-nah may-sah*)

I want to reserve a table, quiero reservar una mesa (*kee-****ehr***-*oh ray-sehr-****bar*** *oo-nah may-sah*)
for one, para uno (1) (***oo***-*no*), dos (2) (*dohs*), tres (3) (*trays*), cuatro (4) (***kwah***-*troh*), cinco (5) (***theen***-*koh*), seis (6) (*says*), siete (7) (*see-****eh***-*tay*), ocho (8) (*oh-choh*), nueve (9) (*n'****weh***-*bay*), diez (10) (*dee-****ayth***)
now, ahora (*ah-****oh***-*ra*)
today, hoy (*oy*)
tomorrow, mañana (*mahn-****yah***-*nah*)
outside, a fuera (*ah-****fwaira***)
inside, dentro (*dentro*)
no smoking, no fumadores (*no foo-mah-****doh***-*rays*)

a mistake (error), un error (*oon her-****ror***)
is service included?, ¿está el servicio incluido? (*ay-****stah*** *ehl sehr-bee-thee-oh een-kloo-****ee***-*doh*) or ¿está incluida la propina? (*ay-****stah*** *een-kloo-****ee***-*dah la proh-****pee***-*nah*)
credit card, tarjeta de crédito (*tar-****hay***-*tah day* ***kray***-*dee-toh*)
what is this?, ¿qué es esto? (*kay ays ****ay***-*stoh*)
I did not order this, no ordené esto (*no or-day-****nay*** ***ay***-*stoh*)
this is, esto es (***ay***-*stoh ays*)
cold, frío(a) (***free***-*oh*)
undercooked, crudo (***kroo***-*doh*)
overcooked, muy hecho (***moo***-*ee* ***ay***-*choh*)
delicious, delicioso (*day-lee-thee-****oh***-*soh*)

cheap/expensive, barato(a)/caro(a) (*bah-**rah**-toh/**kah**-roh*)
good/bad, bueno(a)/malo(a) (*bway-no/**mah**-loh*)
less/more, menos/más (*may nohs/mahs*)
the same, el mismo (*ehl **mees**-moh*)
another, otro (*oh-troh*)

I am drunk, soy borracho (*soy boh-**rah**-choh*)
I am a vegetarian, soy vegetariano(a) (*soy bay-hay-tah-ree-**ah**-noh*)
I am diabetic, soy diabético(a) (*soy dee-ah-**bay**-tee-koh*))
without meat, sin carne (*seen **car**-nay*)
without seafood, sin mariscos (*seen mah-**ree**-skohs*)
without pork, sin cerdo (*seen **thehr**-doh*)
without sugar, sin azúcar (*seen ath-**oo**-car*)

open, abierto (*ah-bee-**yehr**-toh*)
closed, cerrado (*thehr-**rah**-doh*)

Monday, lunes (***loo**-nays*)
Tuesday, martes (***mar**-tays*)
Wednesday, miércoles (*mee-**ehr**-koh-lays*)
Thursday, jueves (***hway**-bays*)
Friday, viernes (*bee-**ehr**-nays*)
Saturday, sábado (***sah**-bah-doh*)
Sunday, domingo (*doh-**meen**-goh*)

8. INDEX

AIRPORT 97
Alcázar (Toledo) 63
amusement park 57
Antiguo Barrio Judio (Toledo) 61
antiques 93
apartment rental 83
archeology museum 52
Arco de la Victoria 57
arrival 97
ATM 98
Atocha station 47
AVE high-speed train 97-98

BANCO DE ESPAÑA 48
banking 98
ballet 21, 33, 71
Biblioteca Nacional 52
botanic garden 18, 29, 46, 79
budget dining 92
bullfighting 20, 95
bus 97
business hours 98

CABLE CAR 57
Calle de Alcalá 48
Campo del Moro 35
car rental 97
Casa de Cisneros 20, 27, 75
Casa de la Villa 20, 27, 75
Casa y Museo de El Greco (Toledo) 61
cathedral 21, 27, 34, 63, 72
Catedral (Toledo) 63
Catedral de Nuestra Señora de la Almudena 21, 27, 34, 74
cell phones 101
Changing of the Guard ceremony 12, 26, 34, 72
chocolate 24, 33
chocolatería 24, 33
Chueca neighborhood 37, 53
climate 98
clothing museum 58

Columbus, Christopher 52
consulates 99
contemporary art 16, 30, 35, 43
convent 19, 38, 40
Convento de la Encarnación 40
Convento de las Descalzas Reales 19, 38
Correos building 48
currency 98
customs 100

DANCE/DANCE CLUB 95
decorative arts museum 47, 48, 56
department stores 93
dining 87-91
discounts 16, 102

EATING 87-91
Edificio la Estrella 49
Edificio Metrópolis 49
El Escorial Monastery 65-66
El Greco's House and Museum (Toledo) 61
El Retiro 18, 29, 46, 79
electricity 99
embassies 99
emergencies 99
Estación de Atocha 47
euro 98

FARO DE MADRID 57
fashion/jewelry & clothing stores 93
fashion museum 58
festivals 99
fine arts museums 47
fitness 96
flamenco 36, 95
flea market 94
food stores 89-90, 93
Franco, Francisco 68-69
Fuente de Neptuno 28, 78

GARDENS 18, 29, 34, 46, 56, 79
gay/lesbian 95-96

INDEX

getting around 97-98
golf 96
Goya's tomb 17, 37, 54
Gran Vía 49
Guernica 16, 28, 30, 35, 44

HEMINGWAY, ERNEST 35, 75
holidays 99
Hospital de Tavera (Toledo) 64
hotels 84-86

ICE-CREAM SHOP 57
Impressionist art 17, 50
insurance 99
Internet access 100

JARDINES DE SABATINI 65
Jardin Botánico 18, 29, 46, 79
Jewish sights (Toledo) 61, 62

LA COLEGIATA 41
language 100, 103-105
LGBTQ 95-96
Lujanes Tower 20, 27, 75

MADRID 7-58, 70-90, 92-96
Madrid hotels 84-86
Madrid nightlife 96
Madrid shopping 52, 93-95
Madrid sights 11-58
Madrid restaurants 87-90
Madrid sports and recreation 96
Madrid *tapas* 80-82, 90
markets 75, 89, 94
mealtimes 83
menu translator 88
Mercado de San Miguel 75
mesones 75
metro 97
military museum (Toledo) 63
modern art 16, 30, 35, 43
monasteries 62, 65-68
Monasterio de San Juan de los Reyes
    (Monastery of St. John of the Kings)
    (Toledo) 62
money 98

Museo Arqueológico Nacional 52
Museo Cerralbo 56
Museo de América (Museum of the
    Americas) 19, 57
Museo de la Real Academia de Bellas Artes
    de San Fernando 47
Museo de Santa Cruz (Santa Cruz
    Museum) (Toledo) 64
Museo del Prado 13, 28, 29, 35, 45, 79
Museo del Traje (Museum of Clothing) 58
Museo Lázaro Galdiano 50
Museo Nacional Centro de Arte Reina
    Sofia 16, 28, 30, 35
Museo Nacional de Artes Decorativas 47,
    48
Museo Naval (Naval Museum) 47
Museo Sefardí (Toledo) 62
Museo Sorolla 50
Museo Taurino 20, 95
Museo Thyssen-Bornemisza 17, 28, 29,
    35, 44, 78
Museo Victorio Macho (Victorio Macho
    Museum) (Toledo) 62
music 95

NATIONAL LIBRARY 52
Naval Museum 47
nightlife 96
Northeast Madrid 50-53
Northwest Madrid 54-58

OBSERVATION TOWER 57
Old Madrid 18, 27, 75
opera 21, 33, 71

PACKING 100
Palacio Buenavista 49
Palacio de Bibliotecas y Museos 52
Palacio de Communicaciones 48
Palacio de Linares 48
Palacio Longoria 53
Palacio Real 12, 26, 33, 71
parks 18, 29, 34, 46, 56, 79
Parque de Atracciones 57
Parque del Oeste 56
Paseo del Arte 13, 16, 17, 28, 35, 43

Paseo del Arte museum pass 16, 102
passport 100
phones 101
phrases, Spanish 103-105
Plaza de Colón 52
Plaza de la Villa 20, 27, 75
Plaza de Oriente 21, 26, 33, 71
Plaza de Santa Ana 22, 31
Plaza de Toros 20, 95
Plaza Mayor 18, 27, 30, 35, 76
Plaza Santa Ana 31, 77, 80-82
porcelain 94
postal services 101
Prado Museum 13, 28, 29, 35, 45, 79
prices 84, 87
public transportation 97
Puerta de Alcalá 49
Puerta del Sol 19, 24, 32, 77

REAL ERMITA DE SAN ANTONIO DE LA FLORIDA 17, 37, 54
Real Fábrica de Tapices 48
Reina Sofía 16, 28, 30, 35, 43
relics/religious art 19, 38, 40, 41, 42
restaurants 87-91
restrooms 101
Retiro, El 18, 29, 46, 79
rose garden 56
Royal Palace 12, 26, 33, 71
Royal Theater 21, 26, 33, 71
royal tombs 67
running/jogging 96

SAFETY 99
Salamanca neighborhood 52
San Antón 42
San Francisco el Grande 41
San Isidro 41
San Jerónimo el Real 42
San Lorenzo de El Escorial 65-68
San Nicolás de los Servitas 40
San Pedro el Leal 41
Santa Bárbara 42
Santo Tomé (Toledo) 61
sculpture 62

shopping 52, 93-95
siesta 102
sleeping 84-86
smoking 101
soccer 96
Spanish phrases 103-105
sports and recreation 96
swimming pool 96
subway 97
synagogues (Toledo) 62

TAPAS 31, 32, 78, 80-82, 83
tapestry 48
taxes 98
taxis 97
Telefónica building 49
Teleférico 57
Teatro Español 22, 77
Teatro Real 21, 26, 33, 71
telephones 101
Templo de Debod 56
Thyssen-Bornemisza, Museo 17, 28, 29, 35, 44, 78
Torre de los Lujanes 20, 27, 75
time 101
tipping 103
Toledo 59-64
Toledo hotels 86
Toledo shopping 52
Toledo sights 59-64
Toledo restaurants 91
tourist information 102
trains 97-98
tropical garden 47

VALLE DE LOS CAIDOS (Valley of the Fallen) 68-69
Viejo Madrid (Old Madrid) 18, 27, 76

WALKS 70-82
water (drinking) 102
weather 98
web sites 102
WiFi 100

If you're traveling to Barcelona, check out our *Barcelona Made Easy* guide (available in paperback and ebook). This handy guide includes the sights and walks of Barcelona.

If you're interested in eating and drinking, we also offer *Eating & Drinking in Spain & Portugal: Menu Translator and Restaurant Guide*. It's also available in paperback and ebook.

Before you know it, you'll be drinking *vino tinto*, eating *tapas* and staying up all night - just like real Spaniards!

Available at
www.eatndrink.com
www.amazon.com

Europe Made Easy Travel Guides

Eating & Drinking Guides
Menu Translators and Restaurant Guides

- *Eating & Drinking in Paris*
- *Eating & Drinking in Italian*
- *Eating & Drinking in Spain and Portugal*
- *Eating & Drinking in Latin America*

Europe Made Easy Travel Guides

- *Amsterdam Made Easy*
- *Barcelona Made Easy*
- *Berlin Made Easy*
- *Europe Made Easy*
- *French Riviera Made Easy*
- *Italy Made Easy*
- *Madrid Made Easy*
- *Oslo Made Easy*
- *Paris Made Easy*
- *Paris Walks*
- *Provence Made Easy*
- *Paris Travel Journal*
- *Italy Travel Journal*
- *Europe Travel Journal*

For a list of all Europe Made Easy travel guides, and to purchase our books, visit www.eatndrink.com

CPSIA information can be obtained
at www.ICGtesting.com
Printed in the USA
LVHW082343151222
735339LV00036B/1843

9 781661 399801